Understanding Computers

Understanding Computers

Paul M. Chirlian

Stevens Institute of Technology

dilithium Press
Portland, Oregon

To Barbara, Lisa, and Peter

© Copyright, dilithium Press, 1978

All rights reserved. No part of this book may be reproduced or utilized in any form or by any means, electronic or mechanical, including photocopying, recording or by any information storage and retrieval system, without written permission from the author.

10   9   8   7   6   5   4   3   2   1

ISBN; 0-918398-15-0
Library of Congress number: 78-60611

Printed in the United States of America

dilithium Press
30 N.W. 23rd Place
Portland, Oregon 97210

Preface

This is a book that describes how computers work. It is written for people who use small computers, are contemplating using them, or who are just generally interested in computers. Starting with the most elementary gates and working up to the complete computer, we discuss all phases of computer development. The binary number system and the way that a computer works with numbers are also considered.

In addition to describing the parts of a computer, we discuss elementary machine language programming and talk about assembler languages and higher level languages. The object of the book, however, is not to teach specific languages but to provide you with an understanding of what the languages are and how they operate in the computer.

We also discuss complete computer systems and present a general description of available equipment. This is presented in a practical way so that you can make intelligent choices about your own equipment.

Although this book is intended for use by individual readers, it can also be used as a text for an elementary course in computers. The exercises at the end of each chapter can be used in such courses or can be used by the individual reader to check understanding of the material.

Much loving and heartfelt thanks are due my wife Barbara, who typed and retyped the manuscript and corrected errors in grammar and punctuation, and who provided me with many helpful suggestions. Loving and heartfelt thanks are also due my daughter and son, Lisa and Peter. Lisa typed and corrected the final draft of the manuscript. Peter proofread the manuscript, made corrections, and provided me with many helpful ideas.

Paul M. Chirlian

Contents

1. **INTRODUCTION**   1
   - 1-1. The Computer and the Things That Can Be Done With It   2
   - 1-2. The Basic Ideas of Digital Computers—The Components of a Digital Computer   4
   - 1-3. Computer Construction—Microprocessors   7

2. **NUMBER SYSTEMS**   9
   - 2-1. The Basic Ideas of Number Systems   9
   - 2-2. Changing From One Base to Another   14
   - 2-3. Some Elementary Binary Arithmetic   19

3. **BASIC COMPUTER ELEMENTS**   25
   - 3-1. Logical Notation   25
   - 3-2. Gates   27
   - 3-3. Interconnection of Gates to Obtain Other Gates   34
   - 3-4. The Adder   37
   - 3-5. The Multiplexer   41
   - 3-6. Flip-flops   43
   - 3-7. Clocking   50
   - 3-8. Registers   52
   - 3-9. Counters   58
   - 3-10. Sequence Detectors and Sequence Generators   61

4. **MEMORIES**   65
   - 4-1. Semiconductor Memories   66
   - 4-2. Paralleling of Memory Devices   72
   - 4-3. Magnetic RAMs   76
   - 4-4. Read Only Memories—ROMs   80
   - 4-5. Tape, Disk, and Drum Memories   83
   - 4-6. Codes   88

5. BASIC DIGITAL COMPUTATION — 93
- 5-1. The Basic Arithmetic Logic Unit — 93
- 5-2. Modular Arithmetic — 97
- 5-3. 2's Complement Arithmetic — 100
- 5-4. Multiplication and Division — 106
- 5-5. Floating Point Numbers — 108
- 5-6. The Arithmetic Logic Unit—ALU — 113

6. THE DIGITAL COMPUTER — 125
- 6-1. The General Organization of a Digital Computer — 125
- 6-2. Memory Commands—Information Transmission — 128
- 6-3. Entering and Execution of Instructions — 131
- 6-4. The Complete Digital Computer — 136
- 6-5. Machine Language Programming — 140
- 6-6. Assembler Language — 151
- 6-7. Loaders — 157
- 6-8. Higher Level Languages — 158

7. COMPUTER APPLICATIONS — 161
- 7-1. Comparison of Computers — 161
- 7-2. Things That Can Be Done with a Computer — 167

8. AVAILABLE SMALL COMPUTERS — 173
- 8-1. Microprocessors — 173
- 8-2. Complete Small Computers — 177
- 8-3. Peripherals — 180

INDEX — 187

1 Introduction

The modern digital computer originally was a device so big that it needed a large room to hold it. In addition, it was expensive, costing over $1,000,000. Because of this size and expense, early computers were owned only by large companies or universities and were only used for large data processing operations.

Technical developments allowed many more people to use these large computers. However, the number of people that could use them was still limited. Computers were usually used to solve the complex mathematical problems of engineers or scientists, or to perform payroll and other data processing operations of large companies.

The original large, expensive computers used vacuum tubes. The introduction of the transistor allowed the development of powerful computers which were physically smaller yet more reliable. However, these computers were still relatively large and expensive. The development of integrated circuits changed all that. Now many transistors and their associated circuitry could be built on a small silicon chip. The cost and size of such complex circuitry was about the same as that of the single transistor built a few years earlier. The present large scale integrated circuits have carried this a step further. Now extremely complex computer circuits can be built on a single silicon chip. This has resulted in very small and relatively inexpensive computers.

A small computer today is within the reach of nearly everyone. Computers are used in cars to control the injection of fuel and by companies to direct many of their operations. Computers are used in all types of instruments to provide immediate information that was not previously available. Individuals who now own their own computers use them to check their finances, play games, and do other operations that are limited only by the inventiveness of the user.

In this book we shall discuss how a computer works and how one can make maximum use of the many available computers. Such an understanding should also enable you to build a computer from the many components that are easily obtainable. In addition to presenting these basic ideas, we shall also discuss many of the simple computers and the types of computer components that are now available.

1-1. THE COMPUTER AND THE THINGS THAT CAN BE DONE WITH IT

Let us look at a computer in operation. An electrical engineer enters specifications for a high fidelity audio amplifier and within seconds the computer prints out the components of the amplifier. Or take the enthusiast who plays chess with the computer. For every move he enters, the computer prints out its move. This process continues until the game is completed, usually won by the computer. In still another case, the manager of a credit department enters a list of customers' account numbers and their monthly purchases and payments. The computer then supplies each customer with a bill based upon these monthly purchases and payments, the past balance, and the service charge.

In all of these examples, it appears as though the computer accepts data, thinks, and then produces some output. Actually, a somewhat different process is taking place. The computer does not "think". It must be *programmed*; that is, it has to be directed to perform a specific set of operations. In all the examples discussed, such a program (series of directions) has been stored in the computer.

Modern computers can store much information. Such stored information consists of both programs to be run and data to be used. For instance, in one of the examples cited, the stored data was the customer's number, name, credit balance, service charge, payments and purchases. In addition, the set of instructions (program) that directed the computer in the printing of the bills was also stored.

The program can direct the computer to perform complex operations using only the basic operations of arithmetic (addition, subtraction, multiplication, and division) and some other relatively simple procedures. For instance, two numbers can be compared and the computer can then determine if they are equal or if one is larger than the other. Using relatively simple procedures, a program can cause complex operations to occur, producing the appearance of thought processes. For instance, if a customer's charge balance exceeds a certain amount, a warning message can be printed on the bill.

In this book we shall discuss how a computer works and show you how one can be constructed using available components. We shall not discuss programming in any great detail. For this, the reader is referred to one of the many programming texts, for example, *Beginning BASIC*, by Paul M. Chirlian, published by dilithium Press, Inc.

The introduction of the *microprocessor* has enabled us to reduce the size of computers and today inexpensive computers can be purchased by individuals who can use them for a variety of tasks or games. For instance, *personal* computers can be used to play games such as chess or checkers; or games that will make an individual imagine that he is traveling through space or exploring caves and undersea caverns.

The owner of a personal computer can use it, just as a business uses a larger computer, to keep track of household finances, taxes, and budgets. In addition, such a computer can be used to control the operation of your house. For instance, heating can be controlled so as to minimize the use of energy. The computer can automatically monitor sensors so that fire and burglar alarms are made more sensitive. For example, with the slightest appearance of light in a dark room at night, an alarm can be automatically triggered.

Some computer applications are in the areas of engineering, science, and mathematics, where it often becomes necessary to solve a set of simultaneous equations having many unknowns. If this were done by hand (or with a simple calculator), the solution would take hours. The computer can perform these calculations in minutes, even seconds. There are, of course, very many other applications of this nature. When radar signals were bounced off the planet Venus, the signals obtained were so weak that they could not be distinguished from electrical noise and interference. Computers were used to perform complex calculations that allowed these signals to be distinguished from the noise. Computers are also widely used by businesses to keep track of accounts, inventory, and daily operations.

We have discussed some of the uses of a personal computer. A thorough understanding of the operation of these computers will show you their capabilities and limitations so that you can devise other uses. Such an understanding is the object of this book.

1-2. THE BASIC IDEAS OF DIGITAL COMPUTERS—THE COMPONENTS OF A DIGITAL COMPUTER

Digital computers operate upon numbers. Sometimes these numbers are codes that can represent program instructions or words such as a person's name. These numbers can also represent actual numbers. For instance, if a person's name is to be supplied to the computer, it is first converted into an appropriate numerical code.

If we are to understand the computer, we must know its number system. We all have worked with the basic *decimal number* system that uses 10 digits. This system was developed because people have 10 fingers. Computers are essentially a collection of electronic switches that are either off or on. In this case, "on" corresponds to one digit, while "off" corresponds to the other. Thus, computers work with a two-digit number system, called a *binary number* system; it uses the digits 0 and 1 (zero and one).

We shall now consider how a digital computer is organized. In subsequent chapters of the book we shall discuss these ideas in greater detail. The terminology used to describe the organization of a computer is not completely standardized. We shall use terminology that is commonly used to describe small computers. The digital computer can be described by the block diagram of Fig. 1-1. We shall now describe each of these blocks in turn.

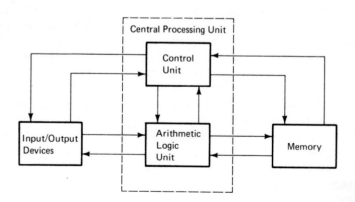

Fig. 1-1. A block diagram illustrating the basic units of a digital computer

Introduction

Arithmetic Logic Unit-ALU

All of the calculations are performed in the *arithmetic logic unit*. This is where the arithmetic operations are performed. For example, two numbers can be added or the size of two numbers can be compared in the ALU.

Control Unit-CU

This unit directs the operation of the computer. For instance, the *control unit* can direct the ALU to add two numbers or to compare the magnitude of two numbers.

Central Processor Unit-CPU

The control unit and the arithmetic logic unit are often called the *central processor unit* of the computer. Note that this notation is not standardized. Sometimes, the ALU is called the CPU.

Memory

All data and programs are stored in the *memory unit*. Actually, there are several types of memory units. The *main memory unit— MMU* is, as the name indicates, the main storage unit of the computer. It is here where the program being run and the data being processed are stored. The main memory usually consists of either semiconductor circuits or magnetic cores. Either type of main memory is sometimes called *core*.

Another component of the main memory is the *read only memory—ROM*. This usually consists of a semiconductor memory that has data permanently stored on it, for example, a table of trigonometric functions. Such data is usually, but not always, incorporated in the memory at the time of its manufacture.

In addition to the MMU, there are also *auxiliary memories*. Such memories store a great quantity of data on magnetic tape or magnetic disks. Such auxiliary memories are cheap, in that they can store a very large amount of data for a reasonable cost. However, the operations of entering or extracting data are slower than those used with semiconductor or magnetic core memories.

Input/Output Devices

A computer would be of no use unless the information supplied to it and the results of its computations can be communicated to the user. This is the function of the *input/output* device. One typical input/output device is the terminal. Here the operator types symbols on a keyboard similar to that of an ordinary typewriter. The terminal then generates electrical signals, in the form of 0's and 1's, that are supplied to the computer. In a similar way, electrical signals are sent from the computer to the terminal. The terminal has a printer associated with it so that these electrical signals from the computer result in the printing of the appropriate data. Instead of a printer, some terminals have a TV screen where the information appears. These are quieter and faster than the printing type but do not produce a permanent copy. This form of input/ouput is often used with small personal computers. The input consists of a keyboard and associated circuitry that generates the appropriate binary code for the computer. The output consists of appropriately wired semiconductor chips that are used in conjunction with an ordinary TV set. Since most people own TV sets, the expense of a screen is eliminated and the cost of the device is reduced since a screen is not required.

Other forms of input/output devices used with large computers are card readers and punches. In this case, cards with punched holes are used to store the input/output information. The card punch has a keyboard similar to that on a typewriter. When a key is pressed, holes are punched in the cards. The positions of the holes determine the symbol (letter, number, etc.) that has been pressed. The card reader obtains the information from the card by sensing the position of the holes. It then sends the appropriate binary information to the computer.

Another form of input/output stores information on a punched tape. Tape punches and readers are often, but now always, associated with Teletypes. When a key on the Teletype is pressed, a set of holes is punched in the tape. The location of the holes corresponds to the desired symbol. When the tape is read, the hole locations are sensed and this information is used to transmit the appropriate electronic signals to the computer.

Another output device is the line printer, which prints an entire line at a time. These devices print at very high speeds and are used when a great deal of data is to be outputted.

Introduction

1-3. COMPUTER CONSTRUCTION—MICROPROCESSORS

The computer circuits in the central processor unit, the control unit, and in the main memory are composed of electronic switches that are either on or off. The earliest electrical computers actually used magnetically controlled switches called *relays*. Relays suffered from two disadvantages; they were relatively slow and they were very large. It would take many milliseconds (thousandths of a second) for a relay to open or close. This may seem fast. However, when most computer programs are evaluated, there may be a sequential opening and closing of billions of these switches. (Note that the same relay may enter into these calculations many times.) Thus, many programs required an extremely long time to run, and since relays were large, computers using relays had to be large also.

In the mid-1940s, the relays were replaced by vacuum tubes which operated as switches. These were much smaller and faster than relays. A fast vacuum tube switch can operate in the order of microseconds (μs). ($1\mu s$ = one millionth of a second = 10^{-6} sec.) Thus, the speed of computers increased tremendously. Vacuum tubes, however, had one great disadvantage: they burned out regularly and had to be replaced. And since a large computer had an extremely large number of vacuum tubes, the likelihood of a tube's failure and the subsequent breakdown of the computer was very high.

In the 1950s and 1960s, computers using transistors in place of the vacuum tubes were developed. Transistors are much smaller than vacuum tubes. In addition, fast transistors switch much more rapidly than vacuum tubes and they do not burn out. With these small and very fast devices, having switching times on the order of nanoseconds (10^{-9} seconds), the modern computer came into its own. This speed allowed long and complex programs to be run in a reasonable time. Short programs could be run very rapidly. This development also brought about the practical use of *time-sharing* where many people seem to use the computer simultaneously. Actually, in a timeshared computer, only one person uses the computer at a time. However, it switches so rapidly between users that it apppears to each user that he alone is using it.

In some large computers, you will often find that the main memory unit uses magnetic devices instead of transistors. Magnetic materials are magnetized by placing them close to an electric current. When the current is removed, some magnetism remains. Thus, data can be stored. This property is utilized in many types of memories and will be discussed in a subsequent chapter. Memories using semiconductor circuits are being built and are gradually replacing magnetic memories in many applications.

The development of integrated circuits greatly reduced the size of computers as well as their cost. Integrated circuits are semiconductor devices. Using optical techniques, many thousands of components such as transistors or resistors can be fabricated on a small chip of silicon. These individual components do not have to be wired by hand as do transistors and vacuum tubes. Consequently, both cost and labor time are reduced, and the manufacture of very small computers becomes a reality.

The first integrated circuit contained only several components such as transistors and resistors. Next came *medium scale integration* (MSI), where 50 to 100 components were fabricated on a single chip. *Large scale integration* (LSI), the fabrication of many thousands of components on a single chip, was a significant step forward. The *microprocessor*, for example, is a direct result of the development of LSI. The microprocessor is a "computer on a chip," actually consisting of the control unit and the central processor which are usually fabricated on a single chip. Microprocessors are relatively inexpensive and have led to the development of the computer hobbyist market, the introduction of the computer into consumer products, such as video games, and the use of the computer in various types of instrumentation and control devices.

EXERCISES

1-1. Discuss the types of tasks or activities that can be performed with computers.
1-2. Discuss the types of activities that you would like to program on a computer.
1-3. What is a program?
1-4. Why is the binary number system used in a computer?
1-5. What is the arithmetic logic unit?
1-6. What is the control unit?
1-7. Describe the function of the main memory unit.
1-8. Describe the function of the auxiliary memory.
1-9. Discuss the various types of input/output devices.

2 Number Systems

We have said that digital computers work with a binary number system using the digits 0 and 1. In this chapter we shall discuss the basic ideas of this number system. In addition, we shall talk about two other number systems that are *not* actually used by the computer but are extremely convenient for the people working with the computer to use.

2-1. THE BASIC IDEAS OF NUMBER SYSTEMS

The number system that we are most familiar with utilizes 10 digits. However, number systems can be formed using any number of digits as long as that number is greater than one. The number of digits used is called the *radix* or *base* of the system. In this chapter, we shall consider the *binary*, or base 2, system; the *octal*, or base 8, system; and the *hexadecimal*, or base 16, system.

To begin our discussion, consider Table 2-1, which compares the various number systems. The hexadecimal system requires 16 digits. It is conventional to use the letters A, B, C, D, E, and F to represent the digits that stand for 10, 11, 12, 13, 14, and 15, respectively. The table will list all numbers that lie between 0 and 36 in radix (base) 10.

In order to know the value of a number, we must first know its radix. To specify the radix, a *subscript* will be added to the number. For example, from Table 2-1, we have

$$12_{10} = 1100_2 = 14_8 = C_{16} \qquad (2\text{-}1)$$

The subscript is *always* written in base 10. Often, when it is clear what base is being used, the subscript will be omitted.

Table 2-1: A Comparison of Number Systems

Radix 10 Decimal	Radix 2 Binary	Radix 8 Octal	Radix 16 Hexadecimal
0	00000	0	0
1	00001	1	1
2	00010	2	2
3	00011	3	3
4	00100	4	4
5	00101	5	5
6	00110	6	6
7	00111	7	7
8	01000	10	8
9	01001	11	9
10	01010	12	A
11	01011	13	B
12	01100	14	C
13	01101	15	D
14	01110	16	E
15	01111	17	F
16	10000	20	10
17	10001	21	11
18	10010	22	12
19	10011	23	13
20	10100	24	14
21	10101	25	15
22	10110	26	16
23	10111	27	17
24	11000	30	18
25	11001	31	19
26	11010	32	1A
27	11011	33	1B
28	11100	34	1C
29	11101	35	1D
30	11110	36	1E
31	11111	37	1F
32	100000	40	20
33	100001	41	21
34	100010	42	22
35	100011	43	23
36	100100	44	24

Number Systems

Let us now discuss some basic ideas of number systems. We shall start our discussion with base 10, since we are most familiar with it. Then we will consider other bases. We shall begin with whole numbers and then talk about fractions.

Consider the number 293_{10}. This indicates

$$2(\text{hundreds}) + 9(\text{tens}) + 3(\text{ones})$$

We can express this in a more compact form using the following:

$$\begin{aligned}10^0 &= 1 \\ 10^1 &= 10 \\ 10^2 &= 10 \times 10 = 100 \\ 10^3 &= 10 \times 10 \times 10 = 1000 \\ 10^4 &= 10 \times 10 \times 10 \times 10 = 10{,}000\end{aligned} \qquad (2\text{-}2)$$

Hence, we can write

$$293_{10} = 2(10^2) + 9(10^1) + 3(10^0) \qquad (2\text{-}3)$$

which means that 293_{10} represents 2 hundreds, 9 tens, and 3 ones. Similarly,

$$32{,}864_{10} = 3(10^4) + 2(10^3) + 8(10^2) + 6(10^1) + 4(10^0) \qquad (2\text{-}4)$$

or, 3 ten thousands, 2 thousands, 8 hundreds, 6 tens, and 4 ones.

Now we discuss the binary number system, which is based on the same ideas as the decimal number system, except that 2_{10} replaces 10_{10}. For instance,

$$101_2 = 1(\text{four}) + 0(\text{twos}) + 1(\text{one}) \qquad (2\text{-}5)$$

Hence,

$$101_2 = 5_{10} \qquad (2\text{-}6)$$

It is convenient here to use the following:

$$\begin{aligned}2^0 &= 1 \\ 2^1 &= 2 \\ 2^2 &= 2 \times 2 = 4 \\ 2^3 &= 2 \times 2 \times 2 = 8 \\ 2^4 &= 2 \times 2 \times 2 \times 2 = 16 \\ 2^5 &= 2 \times 2 \times 2 \times 2 \times 2 = 32 \\ 2^6 &= 2 \times 2 \times 2 \times 2 \times 2 \times 2 = 64\end{aligned} \qquad (2\text{-}7)$$

Hence, we can write

$$101_2 = 1(2^2) + 0(2^1) + 1(2^0) \qquad (2\text{-}8)$$

Similarly, we have:
$$110101_2 = 1(2^5) + 1(2^4) + 0(2^3) + 1(2^2) + 0(2^1) + 1(2^0) = 53_{10} \quad (2\text{-}9)$$

The ideas for octal and hexadecimal systems are similar. For instance,
$$731_8 = 7(\text{sixty-fours}) + 3(\text{eights}) + 1(\text{one}) = 473_{10} \quad (2\text{-}10)$$
Again the following is utilized:
$$\begin{aligned} 8^0 &= 1 \\ 8^1 &= 8 \\ 8^2 &= 8 \times 8 = 64 \\ 8^3 &= 8 \times 8 \times 8 = 512 \\ 8^4 &= 8 \times 8 \times 8 \times 8 = 4096 \\ 8^5 &= 8 \times 8 \times 8 \times 8 \times 8 = 32{,}768 \end{aligned} \quad (2\text{-}11)$$
Thus,
$$4132_8 = 4(8^3) + 1(8^2) + 3(8^1) + 2(8^0) = 2138_{10} \quad (2\text{-}12)$$

The ideas for the hexadecimal base are the same. For instance,
$$1E2_{16} = 1(\text{two hundred fifty-sixes}) + 14(\text{sixteens}) + 2(\text{ones}) = 482_{10} \quad (2\text{-}13)$$
Note that $E = 14_{10}$. Now the following is useful:
$$\begin{aligned} 16^0 &= 1 \\ 16^1 &= 16 \\ 16^2 &= 16 \times 16 = 256 \\ 16^3 &= 16 \times 16 \times 16 = 4096 \\ 16^4 &= 16 \times 16 \times 16 \times 16 = 65{,}536 \end{aligned} \quad (2\text{-}14)$$
Then,
$$263A_{16} = 2(16^3) + 6(16^2) + 3(16^1) + 10(16^0) = 9786_{10} \quad (2\text{-}15)$$

Fractional Parts

Having discussed whole numbers, let's now examine numbers with fractional parts. Again, we shall start with the decimal system since it is most familiar. We indicate a fractional part of a decimal by a decimal point. For example,
$$0.136_{10} = 1(\text{tenths}) + 3(\text{hundredths}) + 6(\text{thousandths}) \quad (2\text{-}16)$$
The following is useful here:
$$\begin{aligned} 10^{-1} &= 1/10 = 0.1 \\ 10^{-2} &= 1/(10 \times 10) = 0.01 \end{aligned}$$

Number Systems

$$10^{-3} = 1/(10 \times 10 \times 10) = 0.001 \quad (2\text{-}17)$$
$$10^{-4} = 1/(10 \times 10 \times 10 \times 10) = 0.0001$$
$$10^{-5} = 1/(10 \times 10 \times 10 \times 10 \times 10) = 0.00001$$

Then, we have

$$0.136_{10} = 1(10^{-1}) + 3(10^{-2}) + 6(10^{-3}) \quad (2\text{-}18)$$

Here is another example:

$$213.3174 = 2(10^2) + 1(10^1) + 3(10^0)$$
$$+ 3(10^{-1}) + 1(10^{-2}) + 7(10^{-3}) + 4(10^{-4}) \quad (2\text{-}19)$$

Now let us consider fractional numbers to other than base 10. The point separating the whole from the fractional part of the number is called the decimal point in the case of base 10. The general name is the *radix point*. In binary, it is called the *binary point*; in octal, it is called the *octal point*; and in hexadecimal, it is called the *hexadecimal point*.

We shall now discuss binary fractions. In analyzing a binary number such as

$$0.101_2 = 1(\text{half}) + 0(\text{quarters}) + 1(\text{eighth}) \quad (2\text{-}20)$$

it is convenient to use the following:

$$2^{-1} = 1/2 = 0.5_{10}$$
$$2^{-2} = 1/(2 \times 2) = 0.25_{10}$$
$$2^{-3} = 1/(2 \times 2 \times 2) = 0.125_{10} \quad (2\text{-}21)$$
$$2^{-4} = 1/(2 \times 2 \times 2 \times 2) = 0.0625_{10}$$
$$2^{-5} = 1/(2 \times 2 \times 2 \times 2 \times 2) = 0.03125_{10}$$

Hence,

$$0.101_2 = 1(2^{-1}) + 0(2^{-2}) + 1(2^{-3}) = 0.625_{10} \quad (2\text{-}22)$$

Similarly,

$$101.1011 = 1(2^2) + 0(2^1) + 1(2^0)$$
$$+ 1(2^{-1}) + 0(2^{-2}) + 1(2^{-3}) + 1(2^{-4}) = 5.6875 \quad (2\text{-}23)$$

The ideas for the octal system are similar, but now it is convenient to use:

$$8^{-1} = 1/8 = 0.125_{10}$$
$$8^{-2} = 1/(8 \times 8) = 0.015625_{10}$$
$$8^{-3} = 1/(8 \times 8 \times 8) = 0.001953125_{10} \quad (2\text{-}24)$$
$$8^{-4} = 1/(8 \times 8 \times 8 \times 8) = 0.000244140625_{10}$$

Hence,
$$0.213_8 = 2(8^{-1}) + 1(8^{-2}) + 3(8^{-3}) = 0.271484735_{10} \quad (2\text{-}25)$$
Similarly,
$$\begin{aligned}216.4172_8 &= 2(8^2) + 1(8^1) + 6(8^0) + 4(8^{-1}) \\ &\quad + 1(8^{-2}) + 7(8^{-3}) + 2(8^{-4}) \\ &= 142.5297851563_{10} \end{aligned} \quad (2\text{-}26)$$
For hexadecimal, the following is convenient:
$$\begin{aligned}16^{-1} &= 1/16 = 0.0625_{10} \\ 16^{-2} &= 1/(16 \times 16) = 0.00390625_{10} \\ 16^{-3} &= 1/(16 \times 16 \times 16) = 0.000244140625_{10} \\ 16^{-4} &= 1/(16 \times 16 \times 16 \times 16) = 0.00001525878906_{10}\end{aligned} \quad (2\text{-}27)$$
Then,
$$1E3.0A1_{16} = 483.0393066406_{10} \quad (2\text{-}28)$$

2-2. CHANGING FROM ONE BASE TO ANOTHER

Having discussed the various number systems and the way in which a computer uses them, we shall now analyze some of the convenient procedures that can be used to change numbers in one base to their equivalent form in another. For instance, we shall be able to express a binary number in terms of its decimal equivalent or express a binary number in terms of its octal equivalent.

As the equations written in the previous section illustrate, we already know how to convert from one number system into base 10. We shall now discuss the other conversions, beginning with the conversion of a decimal number into a binary one. Suppose that we have the decimal number 53_{10} and we want to convert it to its binary equivalent. Let's start by seeing how many 2^0's there are in the number. To do this, we divide the number by 2:

$$53/2 = 26 + \frac{1}{2}$$

The remainder (1) represents the number of 2^0's. Now take the quotient (but *not* the remainder) and divide it by 2. This will give us the number of 2^1's. Thus,

$$26/2 = 13 + \frac{0}{2}$$

Since there is no remainder, there is no 2^1 in the binary representation of 53. Now divide the last quotient by 2:

$$13/2 = 6 + \frac{1}{2}$$

Number Systems

The remainder of 1 indicates that there is a 2^2 in the binary expression of 53. Proceeding as before, we have:

$$6/2 = 3 + \frac{0}{2}$$

Thus, there are no 2^3's in the binary expression of 53. Now divide the quotient by 2:

$$3/2 = 1 + \frac{1}{2}$$

Hence, there is a 2^4 in the expression for 53. Now repeat the procedure. Divide the quotient by 2. This gives:

$$1/2 = 0 + \frac{1}{2}$$

Thus, there is a 2^5 in the expression for 53 and the quotient is now zero. Here the procedure stops. Thus,

$$53_{10} = 110101_2 \tag{2-29}$$

If we compare this with Eq. (2-9), we see that the correct result is obtained. In general, we can use this division procedure to obtain the binary equivalent of any decimal number. Let's illustrate this in another example where we express 75_{10} in radix 2:

$$75/2 = 37 + \frac{1}{2}$$

$$37/2 = 18 + \frac{1}{2}$$

$$18/2 = 9 + \frac{0}{2}$$

$$9/2 = 4 + \frac{1}{2}$$

$$4/2 = 2 + \frac{0}{2}$$

$$2/2 = 1 + \frac{0}{2}$$

$$1/2 = 0 + \frac{1}{2}$$

The binary number is obtained by listing all the remainders in reverse order; that is, the first remainder is the rightmost digit. Thus we have:

$$75_{10} = 1001011_2 \tag{2-30}$$

We have just considered the conversion of a whole number. Now we can examine how a fraction expressed in base 10 can be written in binary. In this case, the process involves multiplication by the radix instead of division. Let us illustrate it be expressing 0.125 in binary. We start by multiplying by 2:

$$0.125 \times 2 = 0.25$$

The nonfractional part of the product is 0. Then, the first digit to the right of the binary point will be a 0. Now multiply the fractional part of the product by 2:

$$0.25 \times 2 = 0.5$$

The nonfractional part of the product is 0. Hence, the next digit to the right of the binary point is also a 0. Again, we multiply the nonfractional part by 2:

$$0.5 \times 2 = 1.0$$

The nonfractional part of the product is 1. Now, the next digit to the right of the binary point is a 1. The remaining fractional part is 0. Hence, the process ends and we have:

$$0.125_{10} = 0.001_2 \qquad (2\text{-}31)$$

Take another example. Express 0.257_{10} in binary and remember that only the fractional part is multiplied by 2:

$$0.257 \times 2 = 0.514$$
$$0.514 \times 2 = 1.028$$
$$0.028 \times 2 = 0.056$$
$$0.056 \times 2 = 0.112$$
$$0.112 \times 2 = 0.224$$
$$0.224 \times 2 = 0.448$$
$$0.448 \times 2 = 0.896$$
$$0.896 \times 2 = 1.792$$
$$0.792 \times 2 = 1.584$$
$$\vdots$$

Then,

$$0.257_{10} = 0.010000011\ldots_2 \qquad (2\text{-}32)$$

Note that this process will repeat itself indefinitely; there is no exact binary representation of this number. That is, there will be an infinite number of terms to the right of the binary point. Thus, the conversion of some decimal fractions to binary ones may result

Number Systems

in some inaccuracy since neither people nor computers can work with an infinite number of terms. This inaccuracy is called *round-off error*. Enough terms should be used so that the inaccuracy becomes negligible.

When converting a number that has both whole and fractional parts, each part is converted separately. For instance, to express 53.125_{10} in binary, we would use (2-29) and (2-31) to obtain:

$$53.125_{10} = 110101.001_2 \qquad (2\text{-}33)$$

If we want to convert a decimal number to octal or to hexadecimal, the same procedure is used except that, in the case of octal, the nonfractional part of the number is divided by 8 and the fractional part is multiplied by 8 (16 is used in the case of hexadecimal). For example, let us convert 31_{10} to octal:

$$31/8 = 3 + \frac{7}{8}$$

$$3/8 = 0 + \frac{3}{8}$$

Then,

$$31_{10} = 37_8 \qquad (2\text{-}34)$$

Let's also obtain 0.125_{10} in octal:

$$0.125 \times 8 = 1.000$$

Hence,

$$0.125_{10} = 0.1_8 \qquad (2\text{-}35)$$

A similar procedure is used for conversion to hexadecimal. For example, 31_{10} is converted to hexadecimal:

$$31/16 = 1 + \frac{15}{16}$$

$$1/16 = 0 + \frac{1}{16}$$

The decimal number 15 is represented by the hexadecimal digit F. Hence,

$$31_{10} = 1F_{16} \qquad (2\text{-}36)$$

Finally, let us convert 0.125_{10} to hexadecimal:

$$0.125 \times 16 = 2.000 \qquad (2\text{-}37)$$

There is no remaining fractional part. Hence,

$$0.125_{10} = 0.2_{16} \qquad (2\text{-}38)$$

The conversion between binary and octal or hexadecimal is relatively simple and can usually be done by inspection. Suppose that we want to convert the octal number 2637_8 to binary. Simply write each *digit* of the octal number as a three digit binary number. When these are written in the order that they occur in the octal number, then the desired binary number has been obtained. For instance,

$$2_8 = 010_2$$
$$6_8 = 110_2$$
$$3_8 = 011_2$$
$$7_8 = 111_2$$

Then,

$$2637_8 = 010\ 110\ 011\ 111_2 \tag{2-39}$$

(Note that if an octal number is 0, 1, 2, 3, 4, 5, 6, or 7, it is the same as the corresponding decimal number. See Table 2-1.) Of course, it is conventional to omit the spaces. The leftmost zero can also be omitted. Hence, we can write:

$$2637_8 = 10110011111_2 \tag{2-40}$$

The same procedure can be used with a number with a fractional part. For instance,

$$2637.126_8 = 010110011111.001010110_2$$

These procedures, of course, can be used to convert from binary to octal. For instance, suppose that we have 1011_2 and we want to convert it to octal. First, zeros are added to the left so that the number of digits is equal to a multiple of three. Then the number in question is written as 001011_2. Finally, we break the digits into groups of three and write the equivalent octal for each group. Thus, we have:

$$001011_2 = 13_8 \tag{2-41}$$

The same method is used if the binary number contains a fractional part. Now we add zeros to the right of the number so that the number of digits to the right of the binary point is a multiple of three. *Note that the zeros added to the right or left of the number are added in such a way so that they do not change its numerical value.* For instance, let's convert 1011.10111_2 to octal. Adding zeros, we have:

$$001011.101110 = 13.56_8 \tag{2-42}$$

The conversion between binary and hexadecimal is very similar

Number Systems

to the previously discussed one except that groups of four binary digits are used. For instance,

$$1EA.26B_{16} = 0001\ 1110\ 1010.0010\ 0110\ 1011_2 \quad (2\text{-}43)$$

Note that conversions between binary, octal, and hexadecimal are *not* subject to roundoff error.

In general, computers work with binary numbers. However, it is easier for people to work with octal or hexadecimal numbers since they have many fewer digits and the conversion from binary to octal or hexadecimal is also easy to perform using a computer. Some computers are constructed so that octal or hexadecimal numbers can be entered and/or outputted. However, the actual computations are performed in binary. In most applications, programming and data entering is done in decimal numbers. Octal or hexadecimal is used when the user needs to study the actual binary numbers within the computer. This is very useful if you are constructing a computer and you want to see if it is functioning properly. These binary numbers, and their octal or hexadecimal equivalents, are also used in certain types of programs which we shall subsequently discuss.

2-3. SOME ELEMENTARY BINARY ARITHMETIC

In this section we shall discuss some ideas of addition using binary numbers. In a subsequent chapter we shall discuss binary arithmetic in great detail when we consider how arithmetic is actually performed by a computer. We shall also discuss some restrictions that result when arithmetic is performed by a computer.

Since we are most familiar with the working of the base 10 numbers, let's begin our discussion of elementary binary arithmetic with a basic exercise in addition. Consider the following example:

$$\begin{array}{r} 12436 \\ + 13253 \\ \hline 25689 \end{array}$$

Each column is added to obtain the desired result. In the example chosen, the sum of each column did not equal or exceed the radix. Thus, there was no carrying from one column to the next. Consider what occurs if there is carrying:

$$\begin{array}{r} \overset{\curvearrowleft\curvearrowleft}{1578} \\ + 2694 \\ \hline 4272 \end{array}$$

The result of the first column addition is 12, which exceeds the radix which is 10 in this case; the 2 is written down while the remaining 10 is carried over into the next column by adding 1. The procedure is repeated. For instance, 100 is added to the third column and so forth.

The same basic ideas apply if the numbers are in a radix other than 10. For instance, here is the addition of numbers in octal:

$$\begin{array}{r} 1253_8 \\ + 4321_8 \\ \hline 5574_8 \end{array}$$

You can see that this addition is correct by converting the octal numbers to decimals.

Now consider addition where there is carrying:

$$\begin{array}{r} \overset{\frown\frown\frown}{1476_8} \\ + 1634_8 \\ \hline 3332_8 \end{array}$$

Consult Table 2-1 to see that $6_8+4_8=12_8=10_{10}$. The 2 is written down and the 10_8 is carried into the second column. Now we add $1_8+7_8+3_8=13_8=11_{10}$. The 3 is written down and the 100_8 is carried into the third column. If this procedure seems more complicated than base 10 addition, it is because we are not familiar with octal numbers and do not know the base 8 addition table.

In binary addition, the same process is used. Here is an example that does not require carrying:

$$\begin{array}{r} 10110_2 \\ + 01001_2 \\ \hline 11111_2 \end{array}$$

and an example which does require carrying:

$$\begin{array}{r} \overset{\frown\frown\frown}{10111_2} \\ + 00011_2 \\ \hline 11010_2 \end{array}$$

Consider the first column. Here we add $1_2 + 1_2 = 10_2$. The 0 is written down and $10_2 = 2_{10}$ is carried into the second column. Here we have $1_2 + 1_2 + 1_2 = 11_2$. The 1 is written down and the $100_2 = 4_{10}$ is carried into the third column. This procedure is then repeated. Note that the rules for addition in binary are exactly the same as those for addition in base 10.

Number Systems

In the next example we shall add binary numbers with fractional parts, following the usual rules for addition:

$$101101.101_2$$
$$+ 000110.001_2$$
$$\overline{110011.110_2}$$

A problem which does not occur when we do addition by hand but *can* occur when we use the computer is illustrated in the following example:

$$10110111_2$$
$$+ 10111001_2 \qquad (2\text{-}44)$$
$$\overline{101110000_2}$$

The two numbers that have been added each have eight digits. A binary digit is called a *bit*. Thus, we have added two eight-bit numbers. Because of the carrying in the leftmost column, the answer has nine bits. This presents no problem when people add numbers. However, in computers, numbers are stored in devices called *registers*. A register can only store a certain number of bits. If the binary number has more bits than can be stored, these "excess" bits will be lost. This can lead to substantial error. Let's further explore how this happens.

A register that can store an eight-bit binary number is diagrammatically represented in Fig. 2-1. (We shall discuss actual register circuits in the next chapter.) The right hand digit is called the *least significant digit* since it has the smallest numerical value of all the digits. In a similar way, the leftmost digit is called the *most significant* since it has the greatest numerical value. Assume, for the time being, that we are working with integers. In Chapter 5 we shall apply these results to numbers with fractional parts.

If the addition results in more bits than can be stored by the register, then the bits which are retained are the least significant bits; that is, the most significant digits are *lost*. Thus, if the addition (2-44) were performed and the result were placed in an eight-bit register, the answer would be

$$01110000_2 = 112_{10}$$

rather than the correct answer:

$$101110000_2 = 368_{10}.$$

This represents a substantial error and is called an *overflow*. The computer builder as well as its user must have a thorough understanding of number storage if errors of this type are to be avoided.

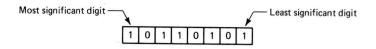

Fig. 2-1. A diagrammatic representation of an 8 bit register storing 10110101_2

In Chapters 4 and 5 we shall discuss binary number storage theory and arithmetic in greater detail as well as the way in which overflow can, at times, be used as an aid in computations.

EXERCISES

2-1. Obtain the values of the numbers from 0_{10} to 36_{10} in base 3.

2-2. Convert the following numbers from base 2 to base 10:
    101,   110011,   101100110.

2-3. Repeat Exercise 2-2 for:
    101.1011,   110011.1011001,   101100110.11001.

2-4. Convert the following numbers from base 8 to base 10:
    173,   1476,   177654.

2-5. Repeat Exercise 2-4 for:
    173.126,   1476.1473,   177654.00172.

2-6. Convert the following numbers from base 16 to base 10:
    1E3,   ABCDEF,   1EC2A1E2B.

2-7. Repeat Exercise 2-6 for:
    1E3.A2,   ABCDEF.ABEC,   1EC2A1E2B.ABCDE.

2-8. Convert the following numbers from base 10 to base 2:
    15,   34,   261,   936,   78423.

2-9. Repeat Exercise 2-8 for the numbers:
    15.316,   34.2681,   261.03,   936.0123,   78423.936.
Comment on any errors that occur.

2-10. Repeat Exercise 2-8, converting the numbers to octal.

2-11. Repeat Exercise 2-9, converting the numbers to octal.

2-12. Repeat Exercise 2-8, converting the numbers to hexadecimal.

Number Systems

2-13. Repeat Exercise 2-9, converting the numbers to hexadecimal.

2-14. Convert the numbers of Exercise 2-2 to octal.

2-15. Convert the numbers of Exercise 2-3 to octal.

2-16. Convert the numbers of Exercise 2-2 to hexadecimal.

2-17. Convert the numbers of Exercise 2-3 to hexadecimal.

2-18. Convert the numbers of Exercise 2-4 to binary.

2-19. Convert the numbers of Exercise 2-5 to binary.

2-20. Convert the numbers of Exercise 2-6 to binary.

2-21. Convert the numbers of Exercise 2-7 to binary.

2-22. Perform the addition $A + B$, where

$$A = 01011.0110_2$$
$$B = 11011.0101_2$$

2-23. Repeat Exercise 2-22 for:

$$A = 1237.416_8$$
$$B = 2394.712_8$$

2-24. Repeat Exercise for:

$$A = A12E.AB3_{16}$$
$$B = EFA3.1A2_{16}$$

2-25. Discuss the nature and consequences of overflow in a register.

3 Basic Computer Elements

Certain circuits comprise the basic building blocks of computers and an understanding of them is an essential step towards understanding computers. In this chapter we shall assume that digital signals (0's and 1's) are applied to the circuits under discussion. In a subsequent chapter we shall see where the signals come from.

We shall also introduce an easy way of talking about these circuits. This will not only make our discussions shorter, but it will also assist you in learning how to hook up computer circuits.

3-1. LOGICAL NOTATION

In a digital computer, all values represent either 0's or 1's. We can say that a value, at any point, is a signal, and that the signal is either a 0 or a 1. We call these values *logical variables*. The name comes from the branch of mathematics called *mathematical logic*. In it, mathematicians are concerned with facts that are either *true* or *false*. With computers, we are concerned with 0's and 1's. In either case, we work with the mathematics of a two variable system, so that much of the theory of mathematical logic is helpful to computer designers. We need not concern ourselves with all the details of mathematical logic. Here we shall consider some simple ideas that will make it easy to talk about computer circuits.

We start by defining a binary variable. This is simply a variable that is either 0 or 1; binary variables are used to represent values within a computer. Let us see why this is convenient. In Fig. 3-1, we show a simple switch. In a computer, such a switch would be built using transistors or other semiconductor devices. Here, for the sake of simplicity, we show it as an ordinary switch. The letter

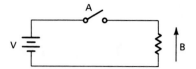

Fig. 3-1. A simple logic circuit

A represents a binary variable. When A = 0, the switch is open, as shown; when A = 1, the switch is closed. The symbol to the left of the diagram is a battery of voltage V. The symbol at the right of the diagram signifies an electrical resistance. It might be convenient to think of it as a light bulb. We can call the whole circuit a *logic circuit*. B represents the voltage across the resistor, and when the switch is open, B = 0. When the switch is closed, voltage appears across the resistor. (The light bulb lights.) We can say that this corresponds to a 1. Thus, for this logic circuit, when A = 1, then B = 1; and when A = 0, then B = 0. We can write this as

$$A = B \qquad (3\text{-}1)$$

There is another way of describing how a logic circuit works. It is called a *truth table*. Here, we list the value of B for all possible values of A. For the logic circuit of Fig. 3-1, we have:

Truth table for Fig. 3-1

A	B
0	0
1	1

B is called the *dependent variable* since it depends upon A. Conversely, A is called the *independent variable*.

Now look at a circuit (Fig. 3-2) that is slightly more complicated. Remember that the switches close when their variables are 1's and open when their variables are 0's. For this circuit, B will be a 1 if

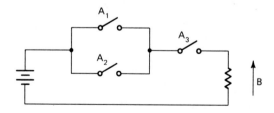

Fig. 3-2. Another logic circuit

Basic Computer Elements

A_1 and A_3 are both 1, or if A_2 and A_3 are both 1, or if A_1, A_2, and A_3 are all 1. The truth table is a convenient way of listing this information. Below are the values for B for all possible combinations of the independent variables, A_1, A_2, and A_3.

Truth table for Fig. 3-2

A_1	A_2	A_3	B
0	0	0	0
0	0	1	0
0	1	0	0
0	1	1	1
1	0	0	0
1	0	1	1
1	1	0	0
1	1	1	1

In this section we have considered some ways of representing logic circuits. Actually, the circuits that we have discussed are called *combinatorial circuits* or *combinational circuits*, and in the next section we talk about some combinational circuits that form the basic building blocks of computers.

3-2. GATES

Circuits are available in integrated circuit form so that you can use them to construct all types of logic circuits. In subsequent sections we shall see how the basic circuits can be used to build many practical digital devices. The circuits that we talk about here perform certain logical operations. We shall discuss their operation and then present the circuit. The circuit that performs the logic operation is called a *logic gate* or more simply, a *gate*.

The AND Gate

An important logic operation is illustrated in Fig. 3-3 which shows two switches connected in what is called a *series* circuit. In

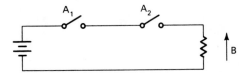

Fig. 3-3. An AND switch circuit

this case, B is 1 only if A_1 *and* A_2 are both 1's. this is called an AND circuit. Its truth table is:

Truth table for the AND operation of Fig. 3-3

A_1	A_2	B
0	0	0
0	1	0
1	0	0
1	1	1

In order to make the writing shorter, special symbols are used to indicate logical operations. For instance, the dot (·) is used to indicate an AND operation. Thus, we can represent Fig. 3-3 by the relation

$$B = A_1 \cdot A_2 \qquad (3\text{-}2)$$

Often, the dot is omitted. For instance, the following is equivalent to Eq. (3-2):

$$B = A_1 A_2 \qquad (3\text{-}3)$$

Semiconductor gate circuits are built that perform such operations as the AND; if the gate does the AND operation, then it is called an AND gate. Instead of using switches to represent gates, symbols which are smaller and more easily drawn are used. The symbol for an AND gate is shown in Fig. 3-4a.

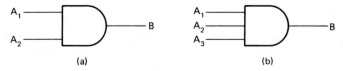

Fig. 3-4. Symbols for the AND gate. (a) Two input; (b) Three input

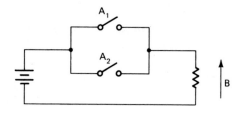

Fig. 3-5. A switch circuit illustrating the OR operation

Basic Computer Elements

We have talked about an AND gate with two inputs. Actually, AND gates can be built with many inputs. A three-input AND gate is shown in Fig. 3-4b. The output B is 1 only if A_1 *and* A_2 *and* A_3 are all 1's. That is, if we draw a diagram containing switches to represent this AND gate, it would have three switches in series.

The OR Gate

The OR operation is illustrated by the switch circuit in Fig. 3-5. This consists of two switches connected in what is called a *parallel* circuit. Here, B will be a 1, if A_1 is a 1 *or* if A_2 is a 1, *or* if both A_1 and A_2 are 1's. The truth table for the OR operation is:

Truth table for the OR operation of Fig. 3-5

A_1	A_2	B
0	0	0
0	1	1
1	0	1
1	1	1

The symbol used to designate the OR operation is a +. Thus, for Fig. 3-5, we can write:

$$B = A_1 + A_2 \qquad (3\text{-}4)$$

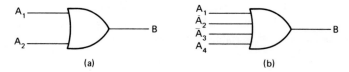

Fig. 3-6. Symbols for the OR gate. (a) Two input; (b) Four input

Note that when logic equations are written, the symbols used are the same as those for ordinary arithmetic. However, *their meanings are not the same.* The symbol for a two-input OR gate is shown in Fig. 3-6a, and the symbol for a four-input OR gate in Fig. 3-6b. Hence, we have:

$$B = A_1 + A_2 + A_3 + A_4 \qquad (3\text{-}5)$$

Now B will be a 1 if A_1 *or* A_2 *or* A_3 *or* A_4 (in any combination) is a 1.

To provide an example of gate circuits, let's represent the switch circuit in Fig. 3-2 by a gate circuit. From Fig. 3-2 we see that B

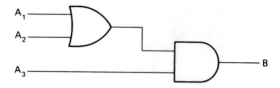

Fig. 3-7. A gate circuit representation of Fig. 3-2

will be a 1 if A_1 OR A_2 is a 1, AND if A_3 is a 1. The gate circuit in Fig. 3-7 functions in this way also. Thus, the circuit in Fig. 3-7 is a gate circuit representation of Fig. 3-2. A logic equation that represents the circuit can be written as follows:

$$B = (A_1 + A_2)A_3 \qquad (3\text{-}6)$$

The interpretation of the parentheses is that all terms within the parentheses are treated as a single variable in relation to the variable outside of the parentheses. Thus, B is a 1 if A_1 OR A_2 is 1, AND if A_3 is a 1.

The NOT Gate—Complements

Let us now consider the logic operation called *complementation*. If A is a 1, then its *complement* is a 0, and if A is a 0, then its complement is a 1. That is, when we take the complement, we change a 0 to a 1 and vice versa. The symbol for the complement is a bar (¯) placed over the variable. Hence, if B is the complement of A, we write

$$B = \overline{A} \qquad (3\text{-}7)$$

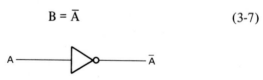

Fig. 3-8. The symbol for a NOT gate

Fig. 3-9. A logic circuit that performs the operation $B = A_1 \overline{A}_2$

Basic Computer Elements

A gate that takes the complement is called a NOT gate. It is symbolically represented in Fig. 3-8. Note that NOT gates have only *one* input. The little circle in the NOT gate symbol is often used to represent a complement operation. For instance, in Fig. 3-9:

$$B = A_1 \bar{A}_2 \qquad (3\text{-}8)$$

In effect, the little circle represents a NOT gate that takes the complement of A_2. Note that the little circle is never used alone, but only in conjunction with other gates.

The NOR Gate

The NOR operation consists of performing the OR operation and then taking the complement of that result. It is defined as

$$B = \overline{A_1 + A_2} \qquad (3\text{-}9)$$

The truth table for the NOR operation is:

Truth table for the NOR operation

A_1	A_2	B
0	0	1
0	1	0
1	0	0
1	1	0

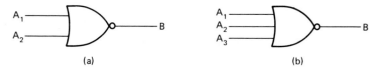

Fig. 3-10. Symbols for the NOR gate. (a) Two input; (b) Three input

Note that B is just the complement of the OR operation.

Symbols for NOR gates are shown in Fig. 3-10. A three-input NOR gate is shown in Fig. 3-10b. Its logical relation is

$$B = \overline{A_1 + A_2 + A_3} \qquad (3\text{-}10)$$

Note that B is 0 when A_1, A_2, A_3, or any combination of them is 1. Actually, NOR gates, and the NAND gates that we shall discuss next, can be very easily built using semiconductor integrated circuits and are generally superior to the other gates. In addition, we shall see that all logic functions can be built using NOR or NAND gates.

The NAND Gate

The NAND operation consists of taking the AND operation and then taking the complement of that result. It is defined as

$$B = \overline{A_1 A_2} \qquad (3\text{-}11)$$

The truth table for the NAND gate is:

Truth table for NAND operations

A_1	A_2	B
0	0	1
0	1	1
1	0	1
1	1	0

Note that B is just the complement of the AND operation. Symbols for the NAND gate are shown in Fig. 3-11. A four-input NAND gate is shown in Fig. 3-11b. Its logical relation is

$$B = \overline{A_1 A_2 A_3 A_4} \qquad (3\text{-}12)$$

Note that B is 0 only when A_1, A_2, A_3, and A_4 *all* are 1's

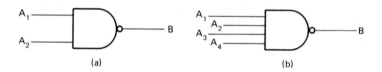

Fig. 3-11. Symbols for the NAND gate. (a) Two input; (b) Four input

Fig. 3-12. The symbol for the XOR gate

The XOR (Exclusive OR) Gate

The exclusive OR operation, which is written XOR or EXOR, is similar to the OR operation except that (for two inputs) the output is 0 if *both* inputs are 1. The symbol for the XOR operation is ⊕.

Basic Computer Elements

Thus, we write the relation for the XOR operation as:

$$B = A_1 \oplus A_2 \qquad (3\text{-}13)$$

The truth table for the XOR operation is:

Truth table for the XOR operation

A_1	A_2	B
0	0	0
0	1	1
1	0	1
1	1	0

The symbolic representation for the XOR gate is shown in Fig. 3-12.

When the XOR gate has more than two inputs, the results are more complicated than those for the other gates. Suppose that we have the following:

$$B = A_1 \oplus A_2 \oplus A_3 \qquad (3\text{-}14)$$

We can write this as:

$$B = (A_1 \oplus A_2) \oplus A_3 \qquad (3\text{-}15)$$

That is, we can take the XOR between A_1 and A_2 and then take the XOR of that result and A_3. (Actually, we can take the XOR between any two variables first. The results will be the same.)

To determine the result of Eq. (3-15), let us use the truth table:

A_1	A_2	A_3	$A_1 \oplus A_2$	$(A_1 \oplus A_2) \oplus A_3$
0	0	0	0	0
0	0	1	0	1
0	1	0	1	1
0	1	1	1	0
1	0	0	1	1
1	0	1	1	0
1	1	0	0	0
1	1	1	0	1

Note that if $A_1 = 1$, $A_2 = 1$ and $A_3 = 1$, then $A_1 \oplus A_2 \oplus A_3 = 1$, and not 0 as might be expected.

We have shown gates with a single lead for each input and output signal. Actually, integrated circuit gates have other terminals (leads). The logical signals consist of voltages which are applied (or measured) between a pair of terminals. One of these terminals, called the *ground* terminal, is common to all inputs and outputs. This common terminal is not shown since we have drawn these diagrams in the conventional way.

In order for these gates (or any integrated circuits) to work properly, they must be connected to a direct voltage such as a battery or a power supply. These power supply terminals are also provided on the integrated circuit chip (but not shown in the logical diagrams). Note that the *correct* power supply voltage must be provided. If it is too small, the circuit will not work properly. If it is too large, the circuit may burn out.

3-3. INTERCONNECTION OF GATES TO OBTAIN OTHER GATES

All of the gate circuits that we have discussed are used in computer circuits. However, all types of gates need not be manufactured since the operation of some gates can be obtained by interconnecting other gates. As an example, consider Fig. 3-13. Here we show how the NOR, NAND, and XOR operations can be obtained from the interconnection of OR, AND, and NOT gates. The NOR and NAND operations just represent the complement of the OR and AND operations, respectively. Thus, these operations can be obtained by connecting the output of OR and AND operations, respectively, to the input of a NOT gate.

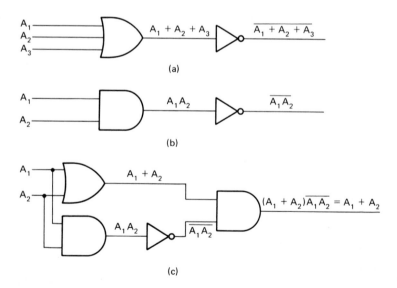

Fig. 3-13. Interconnection of AND, OR, and NOT gates to obtain other gates. (a) NOR; (b) NAND; (c) XOR

Basic Computer Elements

The implementation of the XOR operation is shown in Fig. 3-13c. Here we must use some reasoning to demonstrate that $(A_1+A_2)\overline{A_1A_2}$ is equivalent to the XOR operation. The easiest way to do this is to write a truth table:

A_1	A_2	A_1+A_2	A_1A_2	$\overline{A_1A_2}$	$(A_1+A_2)\overline{A_1A_2}$	$A_1 \oplus A_2$
0	0	0	0	1	0	0
0	1	1	0	1	1	1
1	0	1	0	1	1	1
1	1	1	1	0	0	0

When the next to last column is compared with the last one, which defines the XOR operation, it can be seen that they are the same. Hence, $(A_1+A_2)\overline{A_1A_2} = A_1 \oplus A_2$ and Fig. 3-13c is equivalent to the XOR operation.

Actually, some of the gate circuits that are easiest to fabricate using semiconductor devices are the NOR and NAND gates, and as we shall demonstrate, all gates can be built using only NOR gates or using only NAND gates.

In Fig. 3-14 we show the fabrication of NOT, OR, and AND gates from the interconnection of NOR gates. Figure 3-14a is a two-input NOR gate when both inputs are connected together. Thus, if A = 1, both inputs of the NOR gate will be 1 and its out-

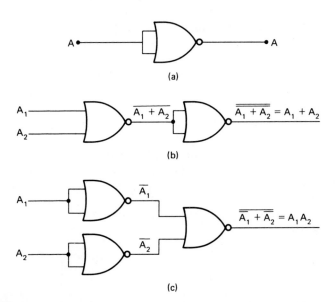

Fig. 3-14. Interconnection of NOR gates to obtain other gates. (a) NOT; (b) OR; (c) AND

put will be a 0. Similarly, if A = 0, both inputs to the NOR gate will be 0 and the output will be a 1. Thus, the output will be the complement of the input and we have constructed the desired NOT gate.

Figure 3-14b represents an OR gate. If we perform the complement twice, the original variable will be obtained. That is:

$$\bar{\bar{A}} = A \qquad (3\text{-}16)$$

The output of the NOR gate is the complement of the OR operation. Hence, taking the complement of the output of a NOR gate results in the OR operation. Note that Fig. 3-14b is just the NOR gate driving a NOT gate. Hence, it results in the OR operation.

Figure 3-14c represents an AND gate. We can show this most easily using a truth table:

A_1	A_2	$\bar{A_1}$	$\bar{A_2}$	$\bar{A_1}+\bar{A_2}$	$\overline{\bar{A_1}+\bar{A_2}}$	$A_1 A_2$
0	0	1	1	1	0	0
0	1	1	0	1	0	0
1	0	0	1	1	0	0
1	1	0	0	0	1	1

When the last two columns are compared, we see that

$$\overline{\bar{A_1}+\bar{A_2}} = A_1 A_2 \qquad (3\text{-}17)$$

Hence, Fig. 3-14c represents the AND operation.

Now let's demonstrate that the NOR, AND, and OR gates can be fabricated from an interconnection of NAND gates as shown in Fig. 3-15.

Figure 3-15a, which shows the NOT operation, is just a NAND gate with all its inputs connected together. Thus, when A = 1, all inputs are 1's and the output is a 0. Similarly, when A = 0, all inputs are 0's and the output is a 1. Hence, the NOT operation has been obtained.

Figure 3-15b represents the AND operation. This can be seen since the NAND operation is the complement of the AND operation. Thus, we take the complement of the complement to obtain the desired result.

It can be demonstrated that Fig. 3-15c is the OR operation by writing the truth table:

A_1	A_2	$\bar{A_1}$	$\bar{A_2}$	$\bar{A_1}\bar{A_2}$	$\overline{\bar{A_1}\bar{A_2}}$	$A_1 + A_2$
0	0	1	1	1	0	0
0	1	1	0	0	1	1
1	0	0	1	0	1	1
1	1	0	0	0	1	1

Basic Computer Elements

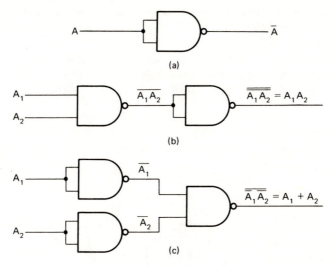

Fig. 3-15. Interconnection of NAND gates to obtain other gates. (a) NOT; (b) AND; (c) NOR

Comaparing the last two columns, we have

$$\overline{\overline{A_1}\,\overline{A_2}} = A_1 + A_2 \tag{3-18}$$

Thus, Fig. 3-15c represents the OR operation.

3-4. THE ADDER

We shall now see how gate circuits can be interconnected to produce a circuit that performs binary addition. Suppose that we want to add two one-bit numbers, a_1 and b_1. The sum is given by:

$$\begin{array}{r} a_1 \\ + b_1 \\ \hline c_1 s_1 \end{array} \tag{3-19}$$

where s_1 and c_1 are each single bits, and s_1 is called the *sum* digit and c_1 is called the *carry* digit. The truth table for this operation is written as follows:

Truth table for the half adder

a_1	b_1	s_1	c_1
0	0	0	0
0	1	1	0
1	0	1	0
1	1	0	1

where the values for s_1 and c_1 are obtained by following the rules for binary addition. (Later, we shall discuss the reasons for calling this circuit a *half adder*.)

Considering s_1 and c_1 separately, let's now construct the gate circuit for this truth table. Let's start with c_1. The circuit should produce a 1 output only when a_1 and b_1 are both 1's. That is,

$$c_1 = a_1 b_1 \tag{3-20}$$

Now look at Fig. 3-16. The output of AND gate c is 1 only when $a_1 = 1$ and $b_1 = 1$. Hence, the output of AND gate c is c_1.

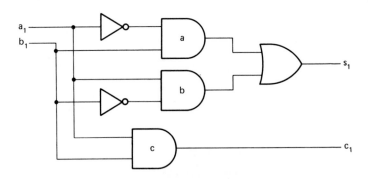

Fig. 3-16. A gate circuit realization of the half adder

Now consider s_1. There are two rows in the truth table with 1's in the s_1 column. Thus, there are two sets of inputs which result in a 1 output for s_1. One set of inputs that should result in an output of 1 is $a_1 = 0$ and $b_1 = 1$. Consider AND gate a. Its inputs are $\bar{a}_1$ and b_1. Thus, its output will be a 1 when $a_1 = 0$ and $b_1 = 1$.

The other set of inputs that result in s_1's being a 1 is $a_1 = 1$ and $b_1 = 0$. Now look at AND gate b. It will only have an output of 1 when $a_1 = 1$ and $b_1 = 0$. The outputs of AND gates a and b are each connected to an input of the OR gate as shown, and the desired output results for s_1. When either $a_1 = 0$ and $b_1 = 1$ or when $a_1 = 1$ and $b_1 = 0$, the output will be a 1. Thus, we can write:

$$s_1 = \bar{a}_1 b_1 + a_1 \bar{b}_1 \tag{3-21}$$

Let us explain this equation again. We want s_1 to be 1 when either

$$a_1 = 0 \quad \text{and} \quad b_1 = 1$$

or when

$$a_1 = 1 \quad \text{and} \quad b_1 = 0$$

Basic Computer Elements

A convenient way of writing this is to consider s_1's being 1 if $a_1 = 0$ and $b_1 = 1$ first. If $a_1 = 0$, then $\bar{a}_1 = 1$. (Remember that a bar over a variable means to take the complement.) Now $\bar{a}_1 \cdot b_1$ will be 1 when $\bar{a}_1$ AND b_1 is 1. This is the same as saying that $a_1 = 0$ and $b_1 = 1$.

In a similar way we can state that $s_1 = 1$ when $a_1 = 1$ and $b_1 = 0$, which can also be expressed as $s_1 = 1$ when $a_1 = 1$ and $\bar{b}_1 = 1$. Thus, the expression for s_1 can consist of an OR operation applied to $\bar{a}_1 b_1$ and $a_1 \bar{b}_1$, which is exactly what Eq.(3-21) is. (Remember that the OR operation is represented by a + sign.) This line of reasoning is also used to arrive at Fig. 3-16.

The half adder can be used to add two binary bits. Suppose that the numbers to be added have many bits. It might seem as though each bit could be added by a separate half adder. However, this is not the case since there may be carrying (see Sec. 2-3). Thus, each adder must have provision for entering the two input bits plus a carry bit from the column to the right. An adder which has such a carry input is called a *full adder*. There will be a full adder for each set of bits to be added. (If we want to add two eight-bit numbers, then eight full adders will be used.) Let's talk about the operation of one of these full adders. Suppose that it adds the jth bit. (If $j = 3$, it adds the third column.) Here we have:

$$\begin{array}{r} c_{j-1} \\ a_j \\ \underline{b_j} \\ c_j s_j \end{array} \quad (3\text{-}22)$$

Note that c_{j-1} is the carry from column number $j - 1$ which is just to the right of the column that we are adding. Using the rules for addition, we can obtain the following truth table:

a_j	b_j	c_{j-1}	s_j	c_j
0	0	0	0	0
0	0	1	1	0
0	1	0	1	0
0	1	1	0	1
1	0	0	1	0
1	0	1	0	1
1	1	0	0	1
1	1	1	1	1

Using the reasoning employed to draw the circuit for the half adder, we obtain the full adder circuit in Fig. 3-17. Each 1 in the s_j column results in an AND gate in the circuit for s_j. Similarly, each 1 in the c_j column results in an AND gate in the circuit for c_j. Since we can write

$$s_j = \bar{a}_j\bar{b}_jc_{j-1} + \bar{a}_jb_j\bar{c}_{j-1} + a_j\bar{b}_j\bar{c}_{j-1} + a_jb_jc_{j-1}, \text{ and} \qquad (3\text{-}23)$$

$$c_j = \bar{a}_jb_jc_{j-1} + a_j\bar{b}_jc_{j-1} + a_jb_j\bar{c}_{j-1} + a_jb_jc_{j-1} \qquad (3\text{-}24)$$

s_j can be realized using four AND gates (each with 3 inputs) connected to a four-input OR gate. Similarly, c_j can be realized using four AND gates connected to a four-input OR gate as shown in Fig. 3-17. We do not need 8 AND gates since s_j and c_j can share an AND gate (the one whose output is 1 when $a_j = 1$, $b_j = 1$, and $c_{j-1} = 1$). This example shows the procedure for reducing the number of gates in a circuit.

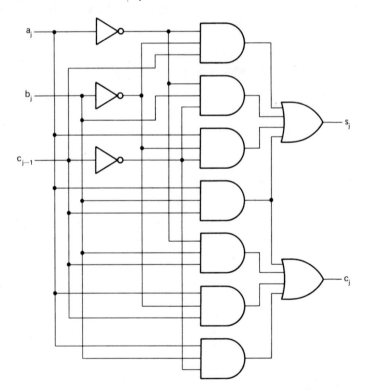

Fig. 3-17. A full adder

Basic Computer Elements

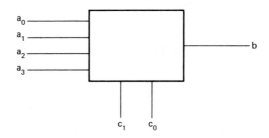

Fig. 3-18. The block diagram for a four input multiplexer

3-5. THE MULTIPLEXER

We shall now discuss a useful circuit called a *multiplexer*, a digitally controlled switch. In Fig. 3-18 we show the block diagram for a multiplexer with four inputs, a_0, a_1, a_2, and a_3, and an output of b. The function of the multiplexer it to connect one of the inputs to the output. This input is specified by a digital signal placed on the control leads c_1 and c_0. The choice is made in the following way. $c_1 c_0$ is used to represent a binary number. For example, if $c_1 = 1$ and $c_0 = 0$, then the number is $10_2 = 2_{10}$. If $c_1 = 1$ and $c_0 = 1$, then the number represented is $11_2 = 3_{10}$. The base 10 value of the base 2 number $c_1 c_0$ indicates the subscript of the input which is to be connected to b. For instance, if $c_1 = 1$ and $c_0 = 1$ ($11_2 = 3_{10}$), then what we want is

$$b = a_3$$

That is, if $a_3 = 1$, then b should equal 1 and if $a_3 = 0$, then b should equal 0.

Let us write a logical expression which expresses the operation of the multiplexer:

$$b = \bar{c}_1 \bar{c}_0 a_0 + \bar{c}_1 c_0 a_1 + c_1 \bar{c}_0 a_2 + c_1 c_0 a_3 \tag{3-25}$$

The expression represents the ORing of four AND operations: $\bar{c}_1 \bar{c}_0 a_0$, $\bar{c}_1 c_0 a_1$, $c_1 \bar{c}_0 a_2$, and $c_1 c_0 a_3$. Because of the OR operation, if any of the AND operations is 1, then b will be 1. (Remember that the bar over the variable indicates that you are to take the complement of that variable.) Now suppose that $c_1 = 0$ and $c_0 = 0$. Then we want $b = a_0$. Consider each of these AND operations:

$$\bar{c}_1\bar{c}_0 a_0 = 1 \cdot 1 \cdot a_0 = a_0 \qquad (3\text{-}26a)$$

$$\bar{c}_1 c_0 a_1 = 1 \cdot 0 \cdot a_1 = 0 \qquad (3\text{-}26b)$$

$$c_1 \bar{c}_0 a_2 = 0 \cdot 1 \cdot a_2 = 0 \qquad (3\text{-}26c)$$

$$c_1 c_0 a_3 = 0 \cdot 0 \cdot a_3 = 0 \qquad (3\text{-}26d)$$

so that, in this case,

$$b = a_0$$

Note that if $a_0 = 1$, then $1 \cdot 1 \cdot a_0 = 1$, and if $a_0 = 0$, then $1 \cdot 1 \cdot a_0 = 0$. Thus, we have achieved the desired result.

Here is another example. Suppose that $c_1 = 1$ and $c_0 = 0$. We want b to equal a_2. Consider Eq. (3-25). Now the first, second, and fourth terms are 0, so that in this case, $b = c_1 \bar{c}_0 a_2$. Since $c_1 = 1$ and $\bar{c}_0 = 1$,

$$b = a_2$$

as desired.

Now let us see how we can build the multiplexer using gates. Equation (3-25) indicates that each AND gate has three inputs. The outputs of the AND gates are $\bar{c}_1\bar{c}_0 a_0$, $\bar{c}_1 c_0 a_1$, $c_1 \bar{c}_0 a_2$, and $c_1 c_0 a_3$. Each output is connected to one input of a four-input OR gate. The diagram for this circuit is shown in Fig. 3-19.

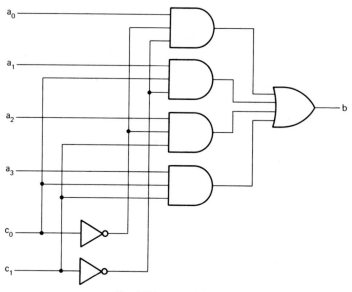

Fig. 3-19. A multiplexer

Multiplexers are used in digital circuits in the same way that switches are used in ordinary electric circuits. Since they can "switch" the output to one of several inputs, they can provide useful functions.

3-6. FLIP-FLOPS

The circuits that we have discussed are called *combinational logic circuits*. In such circuits, the output at any time depends upon the inputs *at that time only*. Hence, these circuits do not have any *memory*; that is, the outputs do not depend upon any *past* inputs or other past values. We shall now discuss circuits that do have memory. These circuits are called *sequential* circuits. In this section we shall discuss some basic sequential circuits called *flip-flops*, which are important building blocks of many larger sequential circuits.

The *flip-flop* or *bistable multivibrator* is a circuit whose output will remain a 0 or a 1 until one or more signals are applied to its input, at which time the output will change. For example, if the output is a 0, it will remain 0 until a suitable signal (or signals) is applied to its input. Similarly, if the output is a 1, it will remain 1 until a suitable input signal (or signals) is applied, causing it to switch to a 0. Since the flip-flop output does not change until these signals are applied, this device can remember a single binary digit (bit).

A block diagram for a flip-flop is shown in Fig. 3-20. Note that there are *two* outputs labeled Q and $\bar{Q}$. As indicated, $\bar{Q}$ will be the complement of Q. In working with computers it is often convenient to have signals which are equal not only to the value of a variable, but also to the value of its complement. (This eliminates the need for many NOT gates.) Thus, almost all flip-flops are built with two such outputs. The value of Q is called the *state* of the flip-flop. If Q = 1, then the state is 1. Similarly, if Q = 0, then the state is 0. Now let us talk about some specific flip-flops.

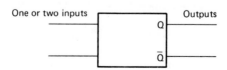

Fig. 3-20. Block diagram of a flip-flop

The R-S Flip-flop

The block diagram for a basic flip-flop, the R-S flip-flop, is illustrated in Fig. 3-21a. If R = 0 and S = 0, then the output does not change. For instance, if Q = 1 ($\bar{Q}$ = 0), then Q remains 1.

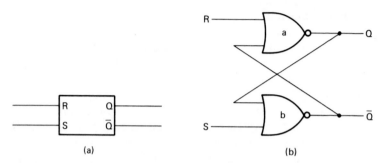

Fig. 3-21. The R-S flip-flop. (a) Block diagram; (b) An implementation using NOR gates

If R = 0 and S = 1, then the state of the flip-flop is set to 1 (Q = 1, $\bar{Q}$ = 0). No matter what the previous state of the flip-flop, after the R = 0, S = 1 input, the state will be Q = 1. If the input is R = 1, S = 0, then the state of the flip-flop becomes 0. No matter what the previous state of the flip-flop, after the input R = 1, S = 0, the state will be Q = 0, $\bar{Q}$ = 1).

The input R = 1, S = 1, is *not allowed*. In general, if you try to apply such an input to an R-S flip-flop, erratic results will be obtained. For example, suppose that you have two R-S flip-flops built by two different manufacturers. They will behave in the same way for all allowed inputs. However, if you apply R = 1, S = 1 to these flip-flops, they may act in different ways. The letters R and S stand for *reset* and *set*. The input R = 0, S = 1 sets the flip-flop to state Q = 1, while the input R = 1, S = 0 resets the flip-flop to state Q = 0.

There are many ways to build flip-flops. An R-S flip-flop constructed using NOR gates is shown in Fig. 3-21b. Let's consider its operation. Suppose that Q = 0 and $\bar{Q}$ = 1, and R = 0, S = 0. One input to NOR gate a will be 1. Hence, Q will remain 0. Both inputs to NOR gate b are 0; hence, $\bar{Q}$ remains 1. Thus, the output does not change.

Now suppose that the input becomes R = 0, S = 1. After this change in input has occurred, one input to NOR gate b is a 1. Hence, its output becomes 0. $\bar{Q}$ becomes 0. Now both inputs to NOR gate a are 0; thus, Q = 1 and the state shifts as it should.

Basic Computer Elements

Now suppose that the input becomes R = 1, S = 0, with the state Q = 1. One input to NOR gate a is a 1 so that Q becomes 0. After this change has occurred, both inputs to NOR gate b become 0 so that $\bar{Q}$ becomes 1. Thus, the correct change of state has occurred.

In a similar way it can be shown that the proper changes of state occur for all allowable combinations of input and output. Note that the changes in Q and $\bar{Q}$ do not occur instantaneously or even at the same time. For instance, suppose that the state is Q = 0 ($\bar{Q}$ = 1) and that the input shifts to R = 0, S = 1. First $\bar{Q}$ changes to 0 and *then* Q changes to 1. In general, these changes take place very rapidly, but not, however, in zero time.

In the computers there are many different circuits, and they do not all respond at the same time. If the computer is to function properly, the correct sequential order of circuit response must be carefully maintained. If we ignore this order, then we may find ourselves trying to use the output of a circuit before it has completed its change in state. There are various techniques used to keep the operation of the computer orderly and to insure that all the circuits respond at proper times.

A very important technique which is used to keep computer circuits in step is called *clocking*. An electronic oscillator circuit called a *clock* generates a pulse train like the one shown in Fig. 3-22. When the pulse is present, the signal level corresponds to a 1; when it is absent, it corresponds to a 0. The flip-flops are usually constructed so that they can only change their state during the time that the clock pulse is present, such as between 0 and T_1, or between T_1 and T_2, etc. Thus, in order to provide for control by a clock, we must modify the flip-flop construction.

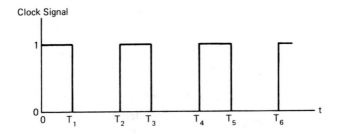

Fig. 3-22. A train of clock pulses

The block diagram for a clocked R-S flip-flop is shown in Fig. 3-23a, and the circuit that actually implements the clocked R-S

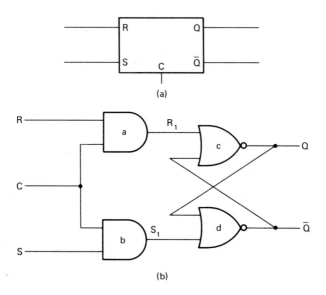

Fig. 3-23. The clocked R-S flip-flop. (a) Its block diagram; (b) A gate circuit realization

flip-flop is shown in Fig. 3-23b. The NOR gates c and d form an ordinary R-S flip-flop whose inputs are R_1 and S_1. Now consider the AND gates a and b. When the clock pulse is absent, the input to C is 0. Thus, the outputs of AND gates a and b will be 0 and $R_1 = 0$ and $S_1 = 0$. Thus, when the clock pulse is not present, the flip-flop cannot change its state.

Now assume that the clock pulse is present. Its signal level is such that it acts like a 1. One input to each of AND gates a and b will be a 1. Consider AND gate a. If C = 1 (the clock pulse is present) and R = 1, then $R_1 = 1$. If C = 1 and R = 0, then $R_1 = 0$. Thus, during those times that the clock pulse is present,

$$R_1 = R$$
$$S_1 = S$$

Then, if inputs are applied during the clock pulse, the flip-flop will change its state and behave like an unclocked R-S flip-flop. When the clock pulse is absent, the flip-flop will not change its state, regardless of the values of R and S. Now let's consider some additional types of flip-flops; we shall assume that they are all clocked.

The D Flip-flop

The D flip-flop is designed with only one input. It is illustrated in Fig. 3-24. If, during a clock pulse, D = 1, then the state of the flip-flop becomes Q = 1 ($\bar{Q}$ = 0). On the other hand, if, during a clock pulse, D = 0, then the state of the flip-flop becomes Q = 0 ($\bar{Q}$ = 1). It may seem as though this type of flip-flop would not be very useful, but as we shall see in Sec. 3-8 there are circuits where its use is very practical.

A D flip-flop constructed using a NOT gate and an R-S flip-flop is shown in Fig. 3-24b. Note that when D = 0, then R = 1 and S = 0. This causes the R-S flip-flop to reset itself to state Q = 0. Similarly, when D = 1, then R = 0 and S = 1. This causes the R-S flip-flop to set itself to the state Q = 1. Thus, Fig. 3-24b is a D flip-flop.

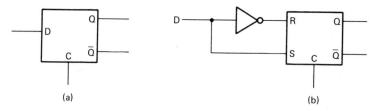

Fig. 3-24. The D flip-flop. (a) Block diagram; (b) Implementation using an R-S flip-flop

The J-K Flip-flop

At times, it is convenient to have a flip-flop that works just like an R-S flip-flop except that the input R = 1, S = 1 is allowed. Such a flip-flop is called a J-K flip-flop. Here the J has the same function as the S, and the K has the same function as the R. When the input J = 1, K = 1 is applied during a clock pulse, the flip-flop changes its state. That is, if Q = 1 and the input J = 1, K = 1 is applied, then the state becomes Q = 0. Similarly, if the state were Q = 0, and J = 1, K = 1 were applied during a clock pulse, the state would become Q = 1.

A block diagram for the J-K flip-flop is shown in Fig. 3-25a, and an actual circuit constructed using an R-S flip-flop and two AND gates is shown in Fig. 3-25b. Let us consider its operation. Suppose that Q = 0, J = 0 and K = 0. The outputs of AND gates a and b will both be 0. Hence, R = 0 and S = 0. Thus, the state remains unchanged (Q = 0).

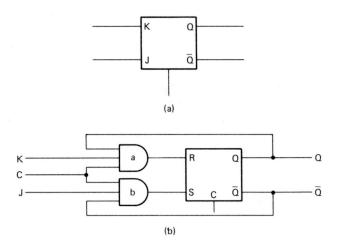

Fig. 3-25. The J-K flip-flop. (a) Its block diagram; (b) Its implementation using an R-C flip-flop and two AND gates

Now suppose that, during a clock pulse, we have $Q = 0$, $J = 1$, and $K = 0$. Then, all inputs to AND gate b will be 1. Hence, $S = 1$. Two inputs to AND gate a will be 0 and, hence $R = 0$. The input $R = 0$ and $S = 1$ causes the flip-flop to set itself to the state $Q = 1$ ($\bar{Q} = 0$). Note that after the change of state has occurred, at least one input to each of the AND gates will be 0 so that the state will not change again.

Next suppose that $Q = 1 (\bar{Q} = 0)$ and that the input during a clock pulse is $J = 0$, $K = 1$. Now all inputs to AND gate a are 1's so that $R = 1$. Two inputs to AND gate b are 0's so that $S = 0$. The input $R = 1$ and $S = 0$ resets the flip-flop to state $Q = 0$. If we continue in this fashion, we can demonstrate that the flip-flop functions properly for all combinations of inputs and outputs.

Now consider the operation of the flip-flop when $J = 1$ and $K = 1$. Suppose that the state is $Q = 1$ ($\bar{Q} = 0$). Then, during the clock pulse, all inputs to AND gate a are 1's. Hence, $R = 1$. Since $\bar{Q} = 0$, one input to AND b will be 0, and hence, $S = 0$. Thus, $R = 1$ and $S = 0$ and the flip-flop will reset itself to state $Q = 0$ ($\bar{Q} = 1$).

Now suppose that the $J = 1$, $K = 1$ input is applied during a clock pulse with $Q = 0$ ($\bar{Q} = 1$). Then, one input to AND gate a will be a 0 while all inputs to AND gate b will be 1's. Hence, we have $R = 0$ and $S = 1$. The flip-flop will set itself to state $Q = 1$ ($\bar{Q} = 0$). Thus, the circuit in Fig. 3-25b will function properly for all inputs including $J = 1$, $K = 1$.

Basic Computer Elements

A problem can arise with the input J = 1 and K = 1. Suppose that the flip-flop can change its state in a time that is much faster than the clock pulse. When the J = 1 and K = 1 input is applied during a clock pulse, the flip-flop changes its state. Since the clock pulse is still present, the flip-flop will change its state again. This may be undesirable. In the next section we shall discuss circuits that eliminate this type of operation.

The T Flip-flop

Another single-input flip-flop is the T flip-flop illustrated in Fig. 3-26. If T = 1 during a clock pulse, then the flip-flop changes its state. If T = 0, then the flip-flop does not change its state. An implementation of the T flip-flop is shown in Fig. 3-26b. It consists of a J-K flip-flop with its inputs connected together. Note that when T = 0, then J = 0 and K = 0 and the state of the flip-flop does not change. When T = 1, then J = 1 and K = 1 and the flip-flop functions as it should.

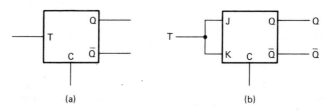

Fig. 3-26. The T flip-flop. (a) Its block diagram; (b) Its implementation using a J-K flip-flop

Preset and Clear Inputs

Integrated circuit flip-flops often have two other inputs called *preset* and *clear*. When a 1 is applied to the preset input, the state of the flip-flop becomes Q = 1 ($\bar{Q}$ = 0). When a 1 is applied to the clear input, the state becomes Q = 0 ($\bar{Q}$ = 1). The preset and clear inputs usually function independently of the clock pulse input and are used to initially set the states of the flip-flops prior to the start of computation.

Some flip-flop preset and clear inputs are operated differently from those we have discussed. Voltage levels corresponding to 1's are continuously applied to the preset and clear inputs. If you want to preset, then the preset input signal is made 0. Similarly, if you want to clear, then the clear input signal is made 0.

3-7. CLOCKING

In the last section we discussed a problem that could arise in a J-K flip-flop with the input J = 1 and K = 1. There, if the flip-flop switching time was faster than the clock pulse time, the output might shift several times during a clock pulse. Similar problems can arise in other computer circuits. For instance, suppose that the output of one flip-flop is the input of another and that a signal is applied to the first flip-flop causing it to change its state; its output changes, and the input to the second flip-flop changes.

Depending upon the speed of operation, and when the input signals were applied to the first flip-flop, the change in the input signals of the second flip-flop can occur at various times. For instance, the state can change well before the end of the clock pulse, or it can occur after the clock pulse has passed; or possibly it can change partially at the end of the clock pulse and partially after it. If the change of the input of the second flip-flop occurs well before the end of the clock pulse, then the second flip-flop will change its state immediately. If the change of the input to the second flip-flop occurs after the clock pulse, then the second flip-flop will not change its state until the next clock pulse has occurred. If the first flip-flop changes its state during the clock pulse but close to the end of the clock pulse, then the second flip-flop may not have time to change its state. The result of all this may be erratic operation; depending upon timing, a flip-flop may or may not change its state at a certain time.

Such erratic operation is not permissible in a digital computer where precise, exact operation is required. We can avoid these problems, however, if the operation of the flip-flop can be properly modified. Suppose that, as before, the flip-flop can only change its state in response to input signals applied *during* the clock pulse. But the output signal of the flip-flop does not change until *after* the clock pulse has passed. Now the difficulties are avoided. For instance, consider the previous example where the output of one flip-flop is the input to the next. During the clock pulse, the output of the first flip-flop does not change; thus, the input to the second flip-flop does not change and the state of the second flip-flop remains the same. After the clock pulse has occurred, for instance, between T_1 and T_2 in Fig. 3-22, the output of the first flip-flop and, hence, the input to the second flip-flop does change. However, the state of the second flip-flop will not change at this time since the clock signal is zero. At the *next* clock

Basic Computer Elements

pulse, the second flip-flop will change its state. Thus, any ambiguity in the operation has been removed. (Note that the first flip-flop cannot change its state until *after* this next clock pulse, so that there is no ambiguity in the input signal of the second flip-flop.)

There are several types of flip-flops that respond in the way that we have discussed. One type is called an *edge-triggered flip-flop*. Another type is called a *master-slave flip-flop*. Let's consider the operation of an R-S master-slave flip-flop. Actually, all the flip-flops can be arranged in this configuration.

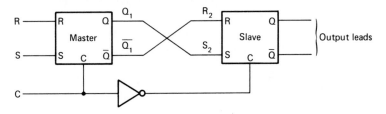

Fig. 3-27. An R-S master-slave flip-flop

The R-S master-slave flip-flop shown in Fig. 3-27 consists of two flip-flops. The output of the first one (the master) is the input to the second flip-flop (the slave). Ignore the clock signal for a moment. The state of the slave flip-flop will always become that of the master. Note that $Q_1 = S_2$ and $\bar{Q}_1 = R_2$. Thus, if the state of the first flip-flop is $Q_1 = 1 (\bar{Q}_1 = 0)$, then we have $R_2 = 0$ and $S_2 = 1$ so that the state of the slave becomes $Q = 1 (\bar{Q} = 0)$. A similar statement can be made if the state of the master is $Q = 0$.

Now consider the effect of the clocking. The clock terminal of the master is connected directly to the clock signal. However, the clock input of the slave is connected to the complement of the clock. During a clock pulse, the master can change its state but the slave cannot since its clock input is 0. Thus, the output does not change. After the clock pulse, the state of the master cannot change. However, now the clock input of the slave is a 1 so that its state can change. Thus, as desired, the output only changes when the clock pulse is not present. In general, when we deal with clocked circuits, we shall assume that they are of the edge-triggered or master-slave forms.

We have now completed our discussion about basic building blocks. Next we shall talk about some very important computer circuits.

3-8. REGISTERS

In this section we shall discuss a circuit called a *register* that is used to store a binary number. That is, it is really a simple memory. In the next chapter we shall talk about large memories. Information is stored in a register, and in all memories, as a sequence of 0's and 1's. In general, this information is supplied to the register in one of two ways. One bit can be inputted to the register on each clock pulse. This is called *series* or *serial input*. If we want to store an eight-bit number, the time for eight clock pulses must elapse. The other type of input is called *parallel input* where all the bits are inputted during a single clock pulse.

The same procedures for the inputting of bits can be applied to the output of information. For instance, suppose that information is to be outputted from a register with serial output. One bit would be outputted on each clock pulse. With parallel output, all of the bits would be supplied during the same clock pulse.

While parallel operation is faster than serial operation, serial operation often results in a saving of equipment. For instance, dialing a telephone is a serial operation. First one number is dialed, then the next, and so on. In parallel operation, there would be a dial for each digit and if we had enough hands, they could all be dialed at once. Similarly, in computers, there are serial adders and parallel adders. In a parallel adder, there is a full adder circuit for each bit (see Sec. 3-4), while in a serial adder, there is only one adder circuit which adds each bit in turn.

The Shift Register

We shall start our discussion of register by considering a serial register called the *shift register*, the operation of which is illustrated in Fig. 3-28. We will first discuss its operation and then consider the circuit implementation. Assume that the shift register can store four bits and that each of the initially stored bits is a 0. Now assume that the first input bit is a 0. Then, after the clock pulse, all bits will still be 0 (Fig. 3-28a). Now suppose that the next input bit is a 1. After the clock pulse, the register will store the contents shown in Fig. 3-28b; that is, the leftmost bit will be the entered 1, while all the other bits will be 0's.

If another 1 is entered, then, after the next clock pulse, the stored contents will be those represented in Fig. 3-28c. In this case, the contents of the register have moved to the right by one bit and the entered bit (1) occupies the leftmost bit position.

Basic Computer Elements

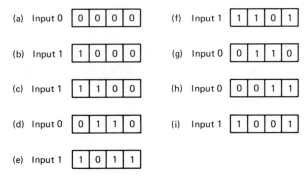

Fig. 3-28. Illustration of the information stored in a four bit shift register on successive clock pulses

Now assume that another 0 is inputted. After the next clock pulse, the contents of the register will be as in Fig. 3-28d; the stored contents all move one bit to the right and the new input bit (0) occupies the leftmost position. Figure 3-28 illustrates the input and serial shifting of nine bits. In the order of their entry, they are 011011001.

With every clock pulse, the information in the shift register shifts one bit to the right. Each time that this happens, the information contained in the rightmost position is lost. It is assumed that this information is used by some other logic circuit in the computer before this occurs.

Now let's see how we can build a shift register. Two simple shift registers are illustrated in Fig. 3-29. One uses J-K flip-flops and the other uses D flip-flops. Consider the register using J-K flip-flops first, assuming at the start that the state of all the flip-flops is 0. Suppose that the first input is a 0. Then $J_1 = 0$ and $K_1 = 1$. Hence, the state of the first (leftmost) flip-flop will remain $Q_1 = 0$ after the first clock pulse. (Note that we assume that master-slave or edge-triggered flip-flops are used here.) Since $Q_1 = 0$ and $\bar{Q}_1 = 1$, then $J_2 = 0$ and $K_2 = 1$. Hence, the state of the flip-flop will not change from $Q_2 = 0$, and similarly, the third flip-flop will not change from $Q_3 = 0$.

Suppose that the next input is a 1. Now we have $J_1 = 1$ and $K_1 = 0$. Then, the state of the first flip-flop will change to $Q_1 = 0$. However, Q_1 will not change its value until after the clock pulse has passed. During the clock pulse, $Q_1 = 0$. Hence, the other flip-flops will not change their states.

When the next clock pulse occurs, $Q_1 = 1$ and $\bar{Q}_1 = 0$, forcing the state of the second flip-flop to become $Q_2 = 1$. However, this

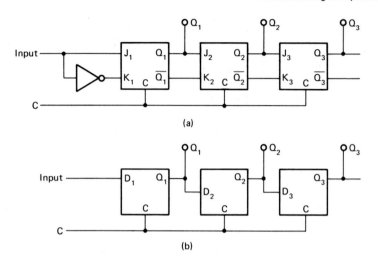

Fig. 3-29. Three bit shift registers. (a) Using J-K flip-flops; (b) Using D flip-flops

output does not occur until after the clock pulse (before this, $Q_2 = 0$). Thus, the state of the third flip-flop does not change. Of course, during this same time, the state of the first flip-flop is established by the input signal.

Proceeding in this way, the information travels to the right with each clock pulse, and the successive inputs establish the state of the leftmost flip-flop.

If Q_3 is taken as the output, then a single bit is outputted with each clock pulse. This is an example of serial output. But if the three leads Q_1, Q_2, and Q_3 are used simultaneously for output, we have a parallel output. Thus, the shift register of Fig. 3-29 can be used for serial input and for either serial or parallel (or both) outputs. If the input is serial and the output parallel, we have what is called a *serial to parallel converter.*

The operation of the shift register in Fig. 3-29b is essentially the same as that in Fig. 3-29a, except that now D flip-flops are used. Remember that the state of a D flip-flop becomes that of its input. If we want to increase the number of bits stored in the register, we need only add additional flip-flops to the right.

In an actual computer, the shift registers are often more versatile than those we have presented here. Let's discuss the design of a shift register that can be controlled to perform several functions. Under normal operation, signals are entered at the left side and are shifted right with each clock pulse, an ordinary operation already discussed.

Basic Computer Elements

We also want to be able to enter the signal at the right side and have the register shift left. In this case, it functions like the ordinary one except that it works from right to left. At times, we may not want the shift register to shift with a clock pulse; that is, we would like the register to retain all its stored information with no changes. We also want to be able to clear the register, to be able to set all its states to 0. Finally, we want to make provision for data to be entered in a parallel, as well as a serial, fashion.

The modes of operation of the flip-flop are controlled by a set of control leads. For simplicity, let us assume that there are four such leads, c_0, c_1, c_2, and c_3. If we want the ordinary shift right, then the signals on the control leads will be $c_0 = 1$, $c_1 = c_2 = c_3 = 0$. If we want the shift left mode of operation, then $c_0 = 0$, $c_1 = 1$, $c_2 = c_3 = 0$. For parallel input, $c_0 = 0$, $c_1 = 0$, $c_2 = 1$, $c_3 = 0$. If we want to clear the register, then $c_0 = c_1 = c_2 = 0$, $c_3 = 1$. If we want no change of stored information on a clock pulse, then $c_0 = c_1 = c_2 = c_3 = 0$.

A circuit for this controlled register is shown in Fig. 3-30. Basically, it consists of the D flip-flop shift register shown in Fig. 3-29b. We shall now discuss how the control signals produce the desired operation. To make it easier to explain the circuit, we have redrawn the diagram for a single stage in Fig. 3-31. This reduces the clutter.

Look at Fig. 3-31. Suppose that all of c_0, c_1, c_2, and c_3 are 0's. Then, all inputs to OR gate e are 0's. Thus, one input to AND gate f is 0. The other input is the clock signal. The output of AND gate f is connected to the C terminals of the flip-flop. Thus, for these control signals, no clock pulse will reach the shift registers. Hence, the contents of the register will not change with a clock pulse. This is the desired operation. If *any* of c_0, c_1, c_2, or c_3 is 1, then the clock pulse will be applied to the C terminal of the flip-flops.

Now suppose that $c_0 = 1$ and $c_1 = c_2 = c_3 = 0$. Then, the output of AND gates b and c will be 0, and the output of AND gate a will be equal to the left input. Thus, this will be the input to the flip-flop. Now consider the complete diagram in Fig. 3-30. For the condition $c_0 = 1$, $c_1 = c_2 = c_3 = 0$, the circuit functions just as the D shift register in Fig. 3-29 did since each flip-flop receives its input from the stage immediately to its left.

Now suppose that we have the input $c_1 = 1$, $c_0 = c_2 = c_3 = 0$. Then, (see Fig. 3-31), one input to AND gates a and c will be 0, and their output will be 0. Since one input to AND gate b is a 1, its output will be the signal on the right input line. Thus, the input

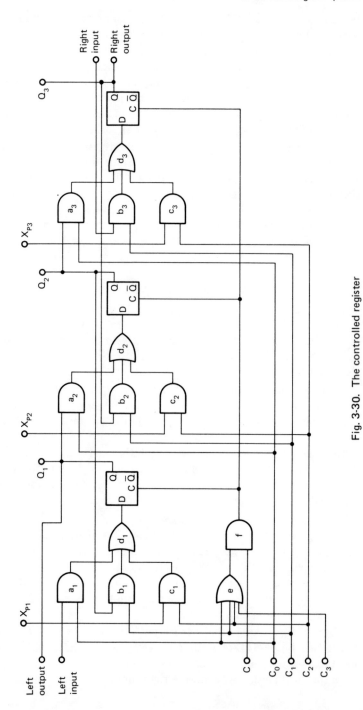

Fig. 3-30. The controlled register

Basic Computer Elements 57

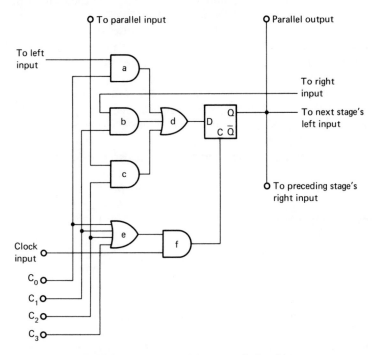

Fig. 3-31. One stage of the controlled register

to the flip-flop is effectively connected to the right input lead. Now look at the complete diagram. If $c_1 = 1$ and $c_0 = c_2 = c_3 = 0$, then this circuit acts just as the D shift register did except that now each flip-flop input comes from the stage to its right. Thus, we have a shift register that enters right and shifts left.

Suppose that the control signals are $c_2 = 1$, $c_0 = c_1 = c_3 = 0$. Using the same reasoning as before (Fig. 3-31), the input of the flip-flop is effectively connected to the parallel input lead. Now consider Fig. 3-30. If the control signals are $c_2 = 1$, $c_0 = c_1 = c_3 = 0$, then the circuit no longer functions as a shift register. Each flip-flop is effectively connected to its own input and stores the signal value on that input line when the clock pulse occurs. Thus, we have a parallel input register. The parallel input leads are marked x_{p1}, x_{p2}, and x_{p3}.

Consider the control sequence, $c_3 = 1$, $c_0 = c_1 = c_2 = 0$. One input to AND gates a, b, and c will be 0 (Fig. 3-31). Hence, the flip-flop input will be 0. Since $c_3 = 1$, whenever a clock pulse occurs, that clock pulse will be applied to the C terminal of all the flip-flops. If the clock pulse is applied with D = 0, then the state of the flip-flop becomes Q = 0. Now consider Fig. 3-30. If c_3 = 1 and $c_0 = c_1 = c_2 = 0$, then, at the next clock pulse, the state of all the flip-flops will become 0. Thus, the register will be cleared as desired.

Having considered all allowable values of control signals and demonstrated that the register functions as we want it to, we shall discuss the output leads. Consider the lead labeled *right output* in Fig. 3-30. It is the output of the rightmost flip-flop. If we shift right and use this lead as the output, the device functions as an ordinary shift register.

In a similar way, if we want the shift register to function as an ordinary shift register but we want it to shift to the left, then the output should be the output of the leftmost flip-flop. Note that in Fig. 3-30, the *left output* lead is shown connected to the output of the leftmost flip-flop.

The output of all the flip-flops are connected to the terminals marked Q_1, Q_2, and Q_3. Thus, a parallel output can be taken at any time. As discussed, there are also parallel input leads, x_{p1}, x_{p2}, and x_{p3}, and the register will function as a parallel input register when c_2 = 1, and $c_0 = c_1 = c_3 = 0$. Note that data can be entered in parallel and then, by switching the control signals to c_0 = 1, $c_1 = c_2 = c_3 = 0$, we can have it outputted serially. Thus, the register can also be used as a *parallel to serial converter*. Similarly, as mentioned, it can also be used as a *serial to parallel converter*.

3-9. COUNTERS

A very useful digital circuit called the *counter* is used to count the number of pulses that are applied to it. Counter circuits are used in computers to keep track of the number of operations that have been performed. They are also widely used in noncomputer applications. For instance, suppose that every person that enters a baseball park passes through a turnstile. Each time that the turnstile turns, a switch is momentarily closed and a pulse is produced. The counter can be used to determine the total number of people in the ball park. Although we have only talked about two of them here, counters are actually used for very many applications.

An actual counter produces a binary number which is equal to the count. Let's discuss a circuit that will count to eight. The next input will cause the counter to reset itself to zero and start all over again. Such a counter is called a *modulo* 8 counter. This type of operation is common to many counters. For instance, an automo-

Basic Computer Elements

bile odometer is a type of counter, counting from 0 to 99999 miles. After the car has traveled one more mile, the odometer will reset itself to 00000.

A circuit for a modulo 8 counter using J-K flip-flops is shown in Fig. 3-32. Assume that the state of all flip-flops has been reset to 0. Note that the input pulses are applied to the C terminals of all flip-flops as well as to the J_0 and K_0 terminals. When the first pulse is applied, $J_0 = K_0 = 1$ during the "clock pulse.". Hence, Q_0 becomes 1 after the pulse. We again assume that master-slave or edge-triggered flip-flops are used here. Thus, Q_0 does not change from a 0 to a 1 until after the pulse has passed. Hence, during the pulse, J_1 and K_1 and J_2 and K_2 are 0. Hence, Q_2 and Q_1 remain 0. The output after the clock pulse is $Q_2 = 0$, $Q_1 = 0$, $Q_0 = 1$; or $001_2 = 1_{10}$, as it should be; that is, one pulse has been counted.

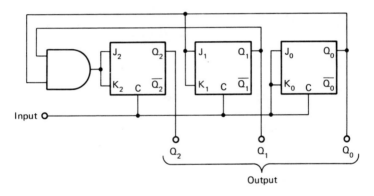

Fig. 3-32. A modulo 8 counter built using J-K flip-flops

When the second pulse is applied $Q_0 = 1$ and the input to the second flip-flop is $J_1 = K_1 = 1$. Hence, Q_1 changes its state after the pulse has passed. In addition, at that time, Q_0 will change from 1 to 0 since J_0 and K_0 also equaled 1 during the pulse. Note that, during the second pulse, $J_2 = K_2 = 0$, since the Q_1 input to the AND gate is 0 until after the pulse has passed. Thus, after the second pulse, we have $Q_2 = 0$, $Q_1 = 1$, $Q_0 = 0$, and $010_2 = 2_{10}$.

When the next (third) pulse is applied, Q_0 again changes its state from 0 to 1 after the pulse. However, Q_1 does not change since, during the pulse, $Q_0 = 0$. During the pulse, the Q_0 input to the AND gate was 0. Hence, $J_2 = K_2 = 0$ and $Q_2 = 0$. Thus, after the third pulse, $Q_2 = 0$, $Q_1 = 1$ and $Q_0 = 1$ ($011_2 = 3_{10}$ as it should).

Now assume that the fourth pulse is applied. During the time that this pulse is present, $Q_2 = 1$ and $Q_1 = 1$. Hence, $J_2 = K_2 = 1$, and Q_2 becomes 1 after the pulse. Since $Q_0 = 1$ during the pulse, then $J_1 = K_1 = 1$ during the pulse. Hence, the second flip-flop will change its state after the pulse. Thus, after the pulse $Q_1 = 0$. Similarly, after the pulse, Q_0 changes to $Q_0 = 0$. Hence, we have $Q_2 = 1$, $Q_1 = 0$, $Q_0 = 0$ ($100_2 = 4_{10}$).

If we continue in this way, we can demonstrate that the counter will count to 8 and then start over again as it should. Counters of this type can be built to count to any power of 2 desired. Other designs can be used to count to any desired number.

At times, we want output in terms of base 10 rather than in terms of base 2. An interconnection of gates in a logic circuit can be used to achieve this. For instance, suppose that we have 8 leads numbered from 0 to 7. Each one represents a particular count. If the count is 2, then the signal level on line 2 should be a 1, while all others should be 0. Similarly, if the count is 6, the signal level on line 6 should be a 1 while all others are 0.

In Fig. 3-32 we show how this could be accomplished. The line representing a count of zero should be the output of a three-input AND gate whose input is $\bar{Q}_2$, $\bar{Q}_1$, and $\bar{Q}_0$. When the count is zero, $\bar{Q}_2 = 1$, $\bar{Q}_1 = 1$, and $\bar{Q}_0 = 1$ and the output of this AND gate will be a 1 as it should. Similarly, the line representing a count of 4_{10} would be the output of a three-input AND gate whose inputs are Q_2, $\bar{Q}_1$, and $\bar{Q}_0$. Proceeding in this way, we can obtain the eight desired decimal output leads.

There is another form of decimal output that can be used. It is called a visual display. For instance, when the count is four, a number four "lights up." In Fig. 3-33, we illustrate the visual element of such a display which consists of seven different straight line segments. When voltages are applied to these segments, they light up. All 10 decimal digits can be formed by lighting the appropriate segments. Actually, there are two commonly used displays. The LED display actually glows and can be read in the dark. The LCD display changes its optical properties when signals are applied to it but it does not emit light. The LED display is very convenient but requires much more power to operate.

Integrated circuits called LED or LCD drivers that contain logic circuits are used to drive these visual displays. Their input leads receive the digital signal from the counter's output. The drivers have seven pairs of output leads, one for each segment in the display. The logic within the driver insures that the appropriate segments in the LED or LCD are activated. For example, if the counter in

Fig. 3-32 has an output of $Q_2 = 1$, $Q_1 = 1$, and $Q_0 = 1$, and this is inputted to an LED driver, then the driver's output would cause the top of the two right hand segments of the LED display to light so that the number 7 would appear.

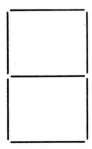

Fig. 3-33. A seven segment numeric display

3-10. SEQUENCE DETECTORS AND SEQUENCE GENERATORS

In this section we shall consider circuits called *sequence detectors*. These circuits will output a 1 if a specified sequence of 0's and 1's is inputted. Otherwise, their output will be a 0. Sequence detectors are not only used in digital computers. They can also be used in things such as digital combination locks. Suppose that you have a radio-controlled garage door opener. It should only open at *your* radio signal, and to no one else's. Your radio transmitter, using a sequence detector, transmits the proper sequence of 0's and 1's, opening the garage door only at your command.

Consider a circuit for a sequence detector that outputs a 1 whenever the sequence 010 is inputted (see Fig. 3-34). Since the flip-flops are master-slave flip-flops, they only respond to signals applied during the clock pulse and only change their outputs after the clock pulse. We assume that one input signal to the sequence detector is applied during each clock pulse. If the input signal level is a 0 during a clock pulse, then a 0 is inputted. Similarly, if the input signal level is a 1 during a clock pulse, then a 1 is inputted.

Now suppose that a 0 has been inputted. Then, at least one input to AND gate b will be 0. Hence, D_1 will be 0. Thus, after the clock pulse, $Q_1 = 0$, $\bar{Q}_1 = 1$. Since the input was a 0, at least one input to AND gate c was also 0. Hence, $D_2 = 0$ so that $Q_2 = 0$. Since one input to AND gate d is a 0, the output is a 0.

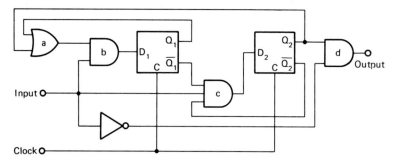

Fig. 3-34. An 010 sequence detector

Suppose that, at the next clock pulse, the input is 1. Now all three inputs to AND gate c are 1's. Hence, D_2 becomes a 1. After the clock pulse we will have $Q_2 = 1$, $\bar{Q}_2 = 0$. Thus, one input to AND gate d will be 1. However, the other input will be 0 since it is the complement of the input. Thus, the output will still be 0.

Now suppose that, during the next clock pulse, the input is a 0. Q_2 cannot change until after the pulse has passed. Thus, during the clock pulse, the lower input to AND gate d will also be a 1 since it is the complement of the input. Hence, the output becomes a 1. If we proceed in this fashion, with all possible sequences, we could show that the output would become 1 whenever the 010 sequence is inputted and at no other time. Thus, this circuit functions as a proper seqeuence detector.

At times, we want to generate a sequence of pulses. This can be accomplished by a device called a *sequence generator.* For instance, such a device would be used in the radio transmitter of the garage door opener. Sequence generators consist of interconnections of flip-flops and gates. The counter in Fig. 3-32 is an example of a sequence generator. If Q_0 is taken as the output, then the sequence 01010... is produced. If Q_1 is taken as the output, the sequence 00110011... is produced, or if Q_2 is taken as the output, the sequence 000011110000... is produced. If we use other interconnections of gates and flip-flops, we can set any desired sequence of 0's and 1's.

EXERCISES

3-1. Write a truth table for the switch circuit in Fig. 3-35.

3-2. Write a truth table for the gate circuit in Fig. 3-36.

Basic Computer Elements

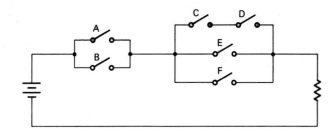

Fig. 3-35.

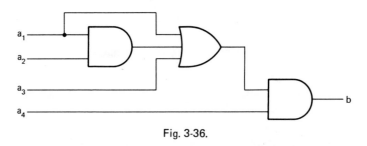

Fig. 3-36.

3-3. Repeat Exercise 3-2 for the gate circuit in Fig. 3-37.

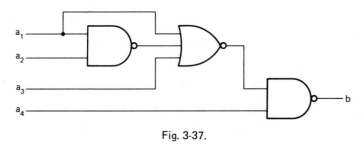

Fig. 3-37.

3-4. Redraw the circuit in Fig. 3-36 using only NOR gates.

3-5. Redraw the circuit in Fig. 3-36 using only NAND gates.

3-6. Obtain a gate circuit which is equivalent to the switch circuit of Fig. 3-35.

3-7. Redraw the circuit in Exercise 3-6 using only NOR gates.

3-8. Redraw the circuit in Exercise 3-6 using only NAND gates.

3-9. Discuss the difference between a half adder and a full adder.

3-10. Discuss how adders are used to add two four-bit binary numbers.

3-11. Write the logic expression for the gate circuit in Fig. 3-36.

3-12. Write the logic expression for the gate circuit in Fig. 3-37.

3-13. Describe, in your own words, the operation of the multiplexer.

3-14. Describe the operation of the R-S, J-K, D, and T flip-flops.

3-15. Describe the operation of the circuit of Fig. 3-21b for all possible combination of inputs and outputs.

3-16. Repeat Exercise 3-15 for the circuit in Fig. 3-23b.

3-17. Repeat Exercise 3-15 for the circuit in Fig. 3-25b.

3-18. Describe the function of the preset and clear inputs of flip-flops.

3-19. Discuss the need for edge-triggered or master-slave flip-flops.

3-20. What is a register?

3-21. What is the difference between serial and parallel operation of registers? Discuss both input and output.

3-22. The following sequence is inputted, one bit per clock pulse, to an eight-bit shift register which initially stores the value 00000000: 1010110011110000111. Describe the operation of the register.

3-23. Completely describe the operation of the register in Fig. 3-29b.

3-24. Completely describe the operation of the register in Fig. 3-30.

3-25. Discuss the operation of the register in Fig. 3-30 as a series to parallel converter.

3-26. Discuss the operation of the register in Fig. 3-30 as a parallel to series converter.

3-27. Describe the operation of digital counters.

3-28. Trace the operation of the counter in Fig. 3-32 through nine counts.

3-29. Draw a logic circuit that will convert from a three-bit binary number to a decimal number that lies in the range 0 to 7. There are to be eight output leads, each one representing a decimal digit.

3-30. Describe some uses for sequence generators and detectors.

3-31. Describe the operation of the sequence detector in Fig. 3-34 for the input sequence 01101010.

4 Memories

All computers have a memory that is used to store both programs and data. In Sec. 3-8 we considered a very simple memory, the register. In this chapter we shall discuss forms of memory that are used to store large quantities of data.

The memory that stores the program that is being run or the data for that program is called the *main memory* or, at times, the *inner memory*. There are other memories called *auxiliary memories*, which are used to store data to be used at a future time. Such memories usually consist of magnetic tapes, drums, or disks. Many programs can be stored on a magnetic tape. When you want to run one of them, it is "read" from the tape and placed in the main memory. In small computers these auxiliary memories are sometimes used as main memories. However, as we shall see, this reduces the speed of the computer's operation.

The memories that we have discussed accept data, and at a later time the data can be read from the memory. There are other forms of memories called *read only memories* (ROMs) where the data is permanently stored and cannot be (easily) changed. Such memory is useful for storing permanent data such as trigonometric tables.

Memories that use semiconductors are fabricated using integrated circuit technology, and are generally very fast and small. Other memories using magnetic materials rather than semiconductors, are slower than the fast semiconductor memories. Magnetic memories have one major advantage over most semiconductor memories in that, in the event of a power failure, magnetic memories do not lose their stored information. They are called *nonvolatile* memories, in contrast to semiconductor memories which do lose their information if the power fails and thus are called *volatile memories*.

Memories are classified by the way that data can be written into them or read from them. The data stored in a memory is organized into groups of bits called words. Each word is stored in a memory location called its *address*. The bits of each word are stored in sequence on a magnetic tape. (This is similar to the storage of tape in an ordinary tape recorder.) Suppose that we want to read the 1500th word and the reading head is positioned over the first word. In order to reach the desired address, the tape must be moved through 1499 words. This is called *sequential access memory*. In general, it is a slow form of memory.

The fastest form of memory is the *random access memory*, RAM, where any memory location can be addressed without having to sequence through any others. Since the reading and writing processes are very fast, RAMs are always used when data access speed is important.

We shall consider all forms of memories in this chapter, starting with a general discussion of random access memories (RAMs).

4.1 SEMICONDUCTOR MEMORIES

Random access memories, which are built using semiconductor circuits, are often used as main memories in computers.

Memories are organized into *words*. Each word consists of a fixed number of bits (0's or 1's). For instance, a word in the memory could be eight bits long. A word could represent a number used in a calculation, or it could represent an instruction in a program. The following might represent a typical operation involving the memory. Two words representing numbers could be taken from two *different* locations in the memory. These could then be added and their sum stored in a third memory location.

The location of a word in a memory is called its *address*. When data is stored in each bit of a word, we say that the word has been *written* into the memory. Similarly, when the data stored in each bit of the word is extracted from the memory, we say that the word has been *read* from the memory. The word which has been written into or read from the memory is said to have been *addressed*.

Although there are actually electronic variations, it is convenient to assume that each bit in a word is stored in a flip-flop; that is, there is a separate flip-flop for every bit that can be stored in the memory. In small computers, words usually contain 8, 16, or 32 bits. In large computers, words may contain 16, 32, 64 or more bits. The memory is usually able to store a large number of words.

The storage of a single bit involves more than just a simple flip-flop. There must be provision for indicating whether information is to be read or written. In general, there is a control lead called a *read/write lead* or *read/write line*. When a logic 1 is placed on this line, the memory will store data. When a logic 0 is placed on the read/write line, the memory will supply (output) data. There must also be provision to address the desired word; that is, when a word is to be read or written, its memory location must be provided. A *memory cell* is the basic unit used to store a bit. In addition to containing the element which actually stores the data, it also has provision for read/write and address signals.

The block diagram for a memory cell is shown in Fig. 4-1a. Note that it has five leads, one for input (for writing data), one for output (for reading data), a read/write lead, an address lead, and a clock input lead.

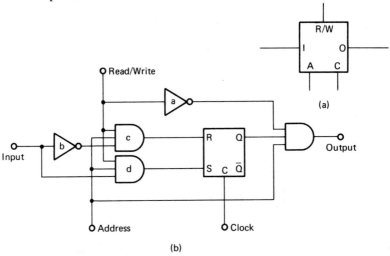

Fig. 4-1. The semiconductor memory cell. (a) Its block diagram; (b) A memory cell that uses an R-S flip-flop

The circuit for a memory cell using an R-S flip-flop is shown in Fig. 4-1b. Let us consider its operation. In order for the circuit to operate, a 1 must be placed on its address line. If this is *not* done, then one input to each of AND gates c, d, and e will be a 0. Then, R = 0, S = 0. Thus, the flip-flop cannot change its state; that is, the memory cell cannot be written on. In addition, the output will be 0. Hence, the contents of the memory cell cannot be read.

Now let us assume that the cell is addressed; that is, there is a 1 on the address line. In addition, assume that the data is to be written into the memory so that there is a 1 on the read/write line.

Thus, two inputs to AND gates c and d will be 1's. Suppose that we want to store a 1 in the memory (write a 1). Then there will be a 1 on the input line. All three inputs to AND gate d will then be 1's. Hence, $S = 1$. However, one input to AND gate c will be a 0. Hence, $R = 0$. Since $R = 0$ and $S = 1$, the flip-flop will, when the clock pulse occurs, set itself to state $Q = 1$. Thus, the 1 will be stored as it should.

If there are 1's on the address and read/write lines and the input is a 0, then $R = 1$ and $S = 0$ and a 0 will be stored in the memory cell.

Now let's assume that we want to read the stored data from an addressed cell. Now there is a 1 on the address line but a 0 on the read/write line. At least one input to each of AND gates c and d will be a 0. Hence, $R = 0$ and $S = 0$ and the stored information will not change. Now two inputs to AND gate e will be 1's while the third will be equal to 0. Thus, the output will equal the data stored in the memory.

An actual memory consists of many memory cells organized into words. In Fig. 4-2 we illustrate a memory composed of four four-bit words. (In general, the number of bits and words will not be equal.) Note the notation used. Subscripts have been added to A, the address lead of the memory cells. These subscripts indicate the word and bit positions that a cell occupies in the memory. For instance, the subscript 1,0 indicates word number 1, bit number 0. Similarly, the subscript 2,1 indicates word 2, bit 1.

Each word is addressed using an address line. Note that all the A leads of the memory cells belonging to the same word are connected together. Thus, if a 1 is placed on address line 0 with 0's on all the other address lines, then all the memory cells for word 0 will be addressed. None of the other memory cells will be addressed. Similarly, if a 1 is placed on address line 2 with 0's on all the other address lines, then all the memory cells for word 2 will be addressed and none of the other memory cells will be addressed. Remember that when a memory cell is not addressed, it does not lose its stored information.

Note that the number of input lines is equal to the number of bits in a word. Since we are using words with four bits, there are four input lines. All of the cells' read/write terminals are connected together. Now suppose that we want to store a (four bit) word in the memory location whose address is 2. Then, a 1 will be placed on both the read/write line and on address line 2 (0 will be placed on all the other address lines). After the next clock pulse, the state of all the flip-flops in word 2 will become equal to the values

Memories

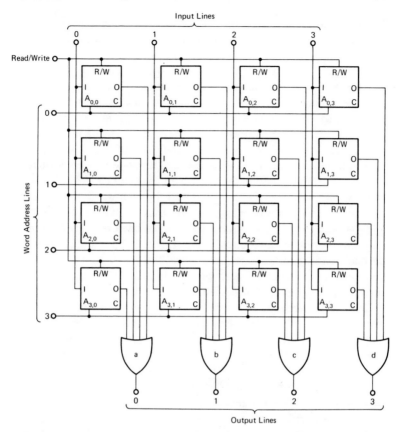

Fig. 4-2. A four word, four bit memory. The clock lead connections are not shown

placed on their respective input lines. Hence, the input four bit word will be stored in address location 2. Note that all the C leads are connected to the master clock line. We have omitted the clock connection from the diagram to avoid clutter.

Now let's see how a word is read from a memory location. There is one output line for each bit in the word. Thus, for this memory, there are four output lines. The output of a memory cell will be 0 unless there is both a 1 on its address lead and a 0 on its read/write lead. Suppose that we want to read word 3. Then, a 1 is placed on address line 3 with 0's on all the other address lines, and a 0 is placed on the read/write line. Now look at OR gate a. It has four inputs, one from bit 0 of each word. However, the output of the 0 bit memory cells of words 0, 1, and 2 will be 0 since these words are not addressed. Hence, the output of OR gate a will be equal to the value stored in bit 0 of word 3. Hence, when a 0 is on the read/write line, the output leads will contain the values of the bits of the stored word which has been addressed.

This type of readout is called *nondestructive* since reading does not remove or *erase* the stored information from the memory; a word will remain stored in the memory until it is written over. A stored word will be unchanged until a 1 is placed on the read/write line and that word is addressed. Now the data on the input leads will replace the previously stored word.

In the memory in Fig. 4-2 there is a separate address lead for each word. If the memory were made on an integrated circuit chip, there would have to be an external lead for each word. Since some memories have a great many words, they would require many address leads. It is undesirable, however, to have very many external leads on an integrated circuit chip. For one thing, the chip must be made large enough to provide for all the connection points and secondly, it increases the cost of the chip. But there are ways of providing many internal leads without introducing these problems.

To reduce the number of *external* leads required, the address is given as a binary number. For example, if there are three binary leads, they can indicate up to eight addresses: 000, 001, 010, 011, 100, 101, 110, and 111. In general, if there are N address lines, then 2^N addresses can be specified. For the four-word memory, we need only use two external leads. If there are more words, the saving is more dramatic. For instance, with 16 external address leads, we can address 65,536 words.

Within the chip, each word must have a separate address lead as indicated in Fig. 4-2. Thus, there must be a circuit in the chip that converts the binary input addresses into signals which are supplied to the internal individual address leads. In Fig. 4-3 we have a circuit that drives four internal address lines from two-bit binary input address lines. The address in binary is supplied on leads a_1 and a_0. The binary number is $a_1 a_0$. If $a_1 = 1$ and $a_0 = 0$, then the address is $10_2 = 2_{10}$. The signals on a_0 and a_1 are used to set the state of the flip-flops D_0 and D_1. After the clock pulse, we will have $Q_0 = a_0$ and $Q_1 = a_1$. Now look at the AND gates. AND gate a will only have an output of 1 if $Q_1 = 0$ and $Q_0 = 0$, that is, if $a_1 = 0$ and $a_0 = 0$. Thus, if the input binary number is $00_2 = 0_{10}$, then internal address line number 0 will have a 1 placed on it. All other address lines will have 0's. Similarly, if $a_1 = 1$ and $a_0 = 0$, then AND gate c will place a 1 on address line 2 ($10_2 = 2_{10}$). All other internal address lines will have 0's. Thus, the circuit in Fig. 4-3, called an *address decoder*, performs the desired function.

Memories

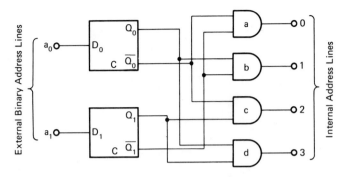

Fig. 4-3. An address decoder. The clock lead connections are not shown

The address decoder in Fig. 4-3 need not contain the flip-flops; they are only used to store the address. In some applications, the binary address may only be present for a short time even though we want to address the memory for a longer time. In such cases, the flip-flops are useful. Note that the clock connections are not shown in Fig. 4-3. It is possible to connect the clock pulses through a control circuit (see Fig. 3-31.) This circuit can be used to apply clock pulses when we only want to change the stored address. If we do not need to store the address, then the two flip-flops can be eliminated from Fig. 4-3. In this case, two NOT gates would be needed to obtain the $\bar{a}_1$ and $\bar{a}_0$ signals.

Cells with Two Address Leads

Some memory cells are built with two address leads. In this case, the circuit in Fig. 4-1b would be modified in the following way. The three AND gates would each have four inputs. The extra input on each gate would be connected to the second address lead. Let's call each cell's address leads A_x and A_y. Note that a cell is not addressed unless *both* A_x and A_y are 1. Such cells can be used in special, very versatile memories which allow single bits to be addressed. The address lead layout for such a memory is shown in Fig. 4-4.

Since each cell is addressed individually, all the cell's input leads can be connected together. Thus, there need only be one external input line. Remember that the input signal will only affect the one cell that has both of its address lines at a logic 1 level. In a similar way, each cell's output lead can be connected to one input of a multi-input OR gate, requiring only one output lead.

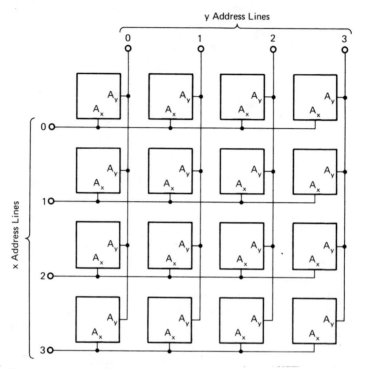

Fig. 4-4. Memory lead diagram for memory cells with two address inputs

The number of external address leads can be reduced by using address decoders as before. In this case, there would be two decoders of the type illustrated in Fig. 4-3: one would drive the x address line and the other would drive the y address line. All of the memories discussed in this section are random access memories, meaning that any word can be addressed without having to sequence through any others.

4-2. PARALLELING OF MEMORY DEVICES

The number of words, or the number of bits per word, in a given memory is often not large enough. However, the capacity of the memory can be increased by adding additional memory devices to form a larger memory. Actually, some memories are sold with a provision to add more memory devices in order to increase capacity. This is called *paralleling of memory devices*. This technique is often used by owners of small computers to increase the size of their memories. In such cases, the memory devices consist of printed circuit boards which have several memory chips and other logic circuitry connected to them. Alternatively, the size of a memory can be increased by adding memory chips to it. This is called *paralleling of memory chips*.

Chip Select Line

Many memory devices that are designed to be paralleled often have an additional external address line called a *chip select line*. This line can be used to turn off the internal address decoder(s) of the memory device. The chip select line functions in the following way. If the signal on the chip select line is a 1, then the address decoder functions just as the one in Fig. 4-3; that is, it uses the external binary address lines to place a 1 on one of the internal address lines.

If the signal on the chip select line is a 0, then the address decoder does not function. No matter what signals are on the external address lines, the address decoder will not place a 1 on any internal address line. The address decoder in Fig. 4-3 can be modified as shown in Fig. 4-5 to have a chip select line. Here we have added an extra input to each of AND gates a, b, c, and d. These extra inputs are connected to the chip select line. When the signal on the chip select line is a 1, then the circuit in Fig. 4-5 functions essentially as does the circuit in Fig. 4-3. On the other hand, when the signal on the chip select line is a 0, then the output of AND gates a, b, c, and d will be 0. Thus, no words on the memory device will be addressed.

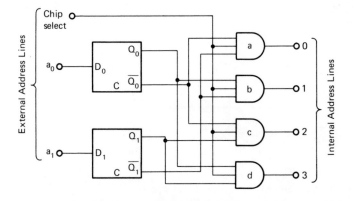

Fig. 4-5. A modification of the address decoder of Fig. 4-3 which includes a chip select input. The clock connections are not shown.

Output Enable Line

Memory devices which are designed to be paralleled often have one address control lead called the *output enable line*. When the signal on this line is a 1, then the memory device functions normally. On the other hand if the signal on the output enable line is a 0, then the output is effectively disconnected from the output lines of the memory device. This is called a *tristate* circuit. In Fig. 4-2, we saw how various outputs can be interconnected using an OR gate. The use of the output enable eliminates the need for the OR gate when the outputs of the memory devices are paralleled. Some memory devices combine the chip select and the output enable lines into a single *chip enable line*.

Now let us see how memory devices can be paralleled to increase the number of words in the memory. In Fig. 4-6. we illustrate the paralleling of three devices. Actually, in this case we assume that each chip contains a memory similar to that in Fig. 4-2 and an address decoder which contains a chip select lead (Fig. 4-5). We assume that the memory device also has an output enable which has been combined with the chip select line into a single chip enable line.

Each memory device contains a four-word, four-bit memory. The a_0 address leads of all the memory devices are connected together. Similarly, the a_1 address lines of all the memory devices are connected together. Thus, signals placed on these address leads will tend to address one word in each of the three memory devices. The chip enable leads are *not* connected together. Thus, only the *single* memory device whose chip enable lead has a 1 signal will actually be addressed. For instance, if we want to address word number 3 of memory device number 2, then we would have the following address signals:

$$a_0 = 1 \qquad (4\text{-}1\text{a})$$

$$a_1 = 1 \qquad (4\text{-}1\text{b})$$

$$CE_1 = 0 \qquad (4\text{-}1\text{c})$$

$$CE_2 = 1 \qquad (4\text{-}1\text{d})$$

$$CE_3 = 0 \qquad (4\text{-}1\text{e})$$

The corresponding input leads are connected together. For instance, all the bit 0 input leads are connected together. Similarly, all the bit 1 input leads are connected together, and all the read/write

Memories

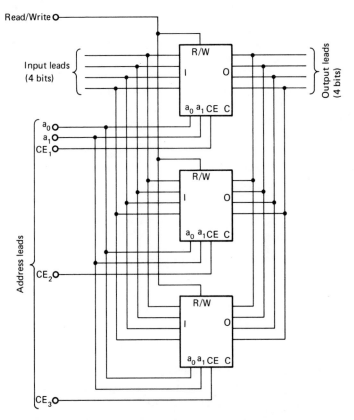

Fig. 4-6. A twelve word, four bit memory constructed by paralleling three four word, four bit memory devices. The clock lead connections are not shown.

leads are connected together. Now suppose that we want to write into word 3 of memory device number 2. The signals given in Eq. (4-1a–4-1e) would be put on the address lines and a 1 would be placed on the read/write line. Then, word number 3 of memory device number 2 has been addressed. Thus, the signal values on the input bit leads would now be stored in the desired memory location.

The corresponding output leads are also connected together. For instance, all the 0 bit output leads are connected. Remember that when the signal on the CE terminal of a chip is 0, the output of that memory device is effectively disconnected. Hence, if we want to read the word stored in address number 3 of memory device number 2, we apply the address signals of Eq.(4-1a–4-1e), and we make the read/write signal 0. Since CE_1 and CE_3 are 0, the outputs of these memory devices are effectively disconnected.

Since $CE_2 = 1$, its outputs are connected to the output line. Thus, the desired word is placed on the output line.

In Fig. 4-6 we illustrated the paralleling of three, four-word memory devices. In general, the memories which are paralleled will contain many more words and the words may contain more bits. Note that there may be variations. For instance, the operation of the control leads, such as chip enable, may vary from manufacturer to manufacturer. Thus, the actual details of the interconnections of the memory device may vary from those discussed, and specific details should be obtained from the manufacturer's data sheets. Although not discussed, memory devices can also be paralleled to increase the number of bits in a word.

4-3. MAGNETIC RAMs

In Sec. 4-1 we discussed a semiconductor memory cell whose basic storage element was the flip-flop. A type of flip-flop can be made using magnetic material. Such "magnetic flip-flops" were, at one time, used almost exclusively as the storage elements in the main memory of large computers. Although they are still used, they are being supplemented by the semiconductor memories in many applications. These magnetic flip-flop memories make use of small, doughnut-shaped magnetic cores for the storage elements. For this reason, the main memories were called *core* memories, and even though cores are not actually used, the name core is still applied, at times, to main memories.

A typical magnetic core is illustrated in Fig. 4-7. Note that this figure is very much larger than an actual core which is several millimeters in diameter. We show the core with a wire through it. When current (i) is passed through the wire, the core becomes magnetized. This is similar to an ordinary electromagnet. If we wrap a coil of wire around a bar of iron and pass a current through the wire, the bar becomes magnetized. Similarly, the core, since it is made of magnetic material, also becomes magnetized when a current i is passed through the wire. Consider the electromagnet. The bar retains some of its magnetism even if the current is removed. The same thing happens to the core.

Figure 4-8 is a graph which shows how the magnetism of the core varies with the current. This type of curve is called a *hysteresis loop*. Note the dashed curve. As the current is increased, the magnetism builds up. After it has reached a certain level, however, there is almost no increase in magnetism with current. In this case, the core is said to have *saturated*. Now suppose that the current de-

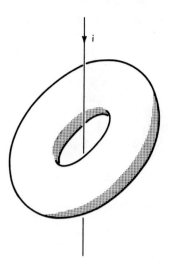

Fig. 4-7. A magnetic core

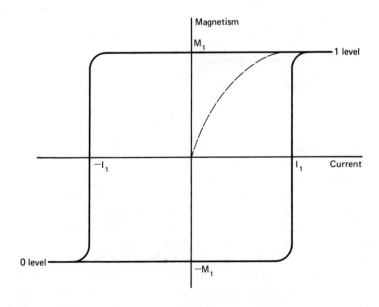

Fig. 4-8. A magnetic hysteresis loop

creases to zero. The magnetism remains almost constant at the level M_1 shown. Even though the current is removed, the magnetism remains. Hence, the core *remembers* that the current was present. Now suppose that we reverse the direction of the current (that is, make it negative). The magnetism remains essentially unchanged until the current almost reaches $-I_1$. Then, the magnetism flips to $-M_1$. Now suppose that the current is increased from $-I_1$ to 0. The magnetism remains at $-M_1$. If the current is increased to I_1, the magnetism will flip again to M_1. Thus, the core functions as a flip-flop. If the magnetism is at level M_1, it stores a 1, while if it is at level $-M_1$, it stores a 0.

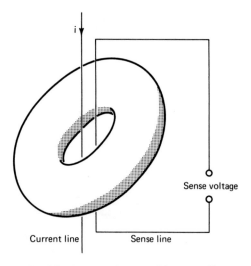

Fig. 4-9. A magnetic core with a sense line

Now let us see how the state of this magnetic flip-flop can be read. If a magnetic field changes near a wire, a voltage will be set up in the wire. The changing magnetic field is said to *induce* a voltage in the wire. Now consider the core in Fig. 4-9. We have passed a second wire called a *sense line* through it. If the core changes its magnetism, a voltage will be induced in the sense line. That is, a voltage will appear at the terminals marked "sense voltage" in Fig. 4-9. Now suppose that we want to read the core. That is, we want to know whether its magnetism is $-M$ or $+M$. We say that we are determining the *state* of the core. Assume that the stored value is a 1, that is, that the magnetism of the core is $+M$. Now suppose that we pass a current $-I_1$ through the current line (Fig. 4-9). This will cause the state of the core to change to $-M$.

Memories

Since the magnetism changes, a voltage will be induced in the sense line. The ouput sense voltage indicates that a 1 was stored in the core.

Now let us consider that a 0 is stored in the core. If we pass a current $-I_1$ through the current line, the magnetism will not change since it is already $-M_1$ and hence, there will be no sense voltage. We have thus determined a way to read the core. In summary, a current $-I_1$ is passed through the current line. If a voltage appears at the sense voltage terminal, then a 1 was stored in the core, while if no output voltage appears, then a 0 was stored in the core.

This form of reading is *destructive*, meaning that, after the core is read, its state will always be a 0. Hence, the stored information is lost. It cannot be read again. This is an undesirable situation and is avoided in the following way. When a word is read from a core memory, it is always stored in a (semiconductor) register. Immediately after it is read, the memory is then set in the write mode and the word stored in the register is written back into the memory. Hence, the stored word is not lost. However, every time that a core memory is read, it must be written on as well. This is a disadvantage since it slows the operation of reading the memory by requiring an extra procedure. Semiconductor memories do not suffer from this problem. On the other hand, semiconductor memories are *volatile* while core memories are *nonvolatile*. Note that if the power is turned off, the information in the core memory will not be lost since the cores will retain their magnetism.

We have illustrated a simple arrangement of a core memory in Fig. 4-9. There is usually more than one current line. For instance, suppose that there are two current lines passing through the core and that the current is smaller in magnitude than $-I_1$ but more than half $-I_1$, for example $-0.6I_1$. This will not be enough to flip the core so that no change in its state takes place if this current is passed through one current line. Now suppose that we put a current of $i = -0.6I_1$ through the other current line. Now there are two currents of $-0.6I_1$ which have the effect of $-1.2I_1$ and the core can change its state. Using two current lines in this way means that the core has two address leads and must be addressed by two different signals. This is analogous to the semiconductor memory cell with two address inputs shown in Fig. 4-4.

When a core memory is constructed, the cores are arranged in arrays similar to that shown in Fig. 4-4. Actually, in the case of core memories, the arrangements are often somewhat more complex than with the semiconductor memories but the ideas are similar.

Magnetic cores are still used in some larger computers, but most of them have been replaced in the small computers by semiconductor memories.

4.4 READ ONLY MEMORIES—ROMs

The memories that we have discussed are designed to have data written into them and to be read from. In turn, new data can be written into the memory and the process repeated. However, there are many applications where we do not want to change the stored data once it has been entered in the memory. That is, this data will be entered once and never changed or re-entered. As discussed in the introduction to this chapter, one application for such a memory is the storage of trigonometric tables. Such memories, whose data is not changed, are called *read only memories*, ROMs. ROMs are also used to perform repetitive operations. For example, suppose that there are ten lines, each one corresponding to a different decimal digit. A ROM can be used to convert these decimal digits into binary numbers. (We shall discuss this application later in this section.)

Read only memories are nonvolatile. The data stored in them is not lost when the power is turned off.

There are several kinds of ROMs. In the ordinary ROM, the information is stored during manufacture. The user of the ROM supplies the data to be stored in it to the manufacturer, and the ROM is built accordingly.

In another form of ROM, the *programmable* ROM or PROM, the user can write data into it once, but then the information is permanently stored and cannot be substantially changed again.

A third form of ROM is called the *erasable* ROM, EROM. Here, the stored values can be erased, often by exposing the ROM to ultraviolet light. However, this erasing and writing is an extremely slow process when compared with the reading of a semiconductor or core memory. Thus, the erasable ROM is almost always used as an ordinary ROM except during rare intervals when it is reprogrammed.

Basic ROM Structure

In order to describe the operation of a ROM, we use the lead structure shown in Fig. 4-10. The actual output lines are called the bit lines. For the time being, consider that the word lines are

Memories

the input lines. A 1 is placed on one and *only* one word line at a time. (The signal levels of the other word lines are 0.) In response to this word line signal, a word is produced on the output line.

To illustrate the operation of a ROM suppose that the ROM in Fig. 4-10 is to perform the following function. It has 10 word lines, each one corresponding to a decimal digit. When a 1 is placed on a word line, its binary value is to appear on the output line. For instance, if a 1 is placed on word line 1, then the output is $a_3 = 0$, $a_2 = 0$, $a_1 = 0$, $a_0 = 1$ ($0001_2 = 1_{10}$). Similarly, if a 1 is placed on word line 6, the signals on the output lines become $a_3 = 1$, $a_2 = 1$, $a_1 = 0$, $a_0 = 0$ ($1100_2 = 6_{10}$).

The circuitry within the ROM connects the output lines to the appropriate word lines. These connections are not ordinarily made with wires but utilize semiconductor circuits that prevent undesirable coupling or connections between input and output circuits.

The actual input to a ROM consists of an address decoder circuit such as that of Fig. 4-3. Now, each internal address line of the de-

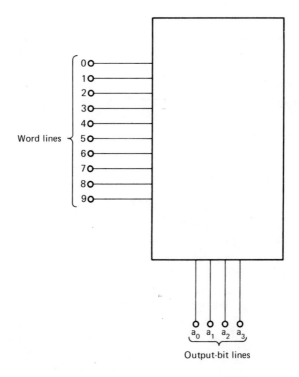

Fig. 4-10. The lead struction of a ROM

coder is connected to a corresponding word line. Then the ROM is treated in the same way as is an ordinary RAM. That is, the ROM is supplied with an address and it produces a word as an output. (Note that the ROM is a form of RAM.)

Programmable ROMs

When a PROM is manufactured, there are connections between all input and output lines. Immediately after manufacturing, if a 1 is placed on any input line, a 1 will occur on all output lines. In such PROMs, there is a *fusable link* placed in series with each coupling. A fusable link acts like a common household fuse. When enough current is passed through it, it melts, opening the circuit. The user then breaks those links where coupling is not desired between the word and bit lines. This is done by passing a large current between input and output line pairs where a connection is not desired. The desired information is now stored.

As an example, suppose that the previously discussed ROM in Fig. 4-10 were a PROM. During its programming all the fusable link connections between input line 0 and the output line would be broken. Hence, no output would result when an input is placed on input line 0. Similarly, the connection between input line 3 and output lines a_3 and a_2 would be broken. Now a 1 placed on input line 3 results in $a_3 = 0$, $a_2 = 0$, $a_1 = 1$, $a_0 = 1$ ($0011_2 = 3_{10}$). Proceeding in this way, the entire PROM can be programmed. Once the PROM has been programmed, it cannot be reprogrammed. Additional fusable links can be broken, but those which have been broken cannot be restored.

Erasable ROMs—EROMs

The coupling between input and output lines in an erasable ROM is a semiconductor circuit which is such that, initially, there is no coupling between the input and output lines. However, if a large current (or, in some cases, a large voltage) is applied between the input and output lines, then these lines are "connected" in an (almost) permanent fashion. EROMs function by trapping a charge in insulating areas. When the large current is applied, the insulating regions temporarily break down. At this point, a charge enters the region. When the large external current is removed, the insulating layer is reestablished, but now a charge is trapped in it. The presence of this charge is used to turn on electronic devices which couple the input and output lines of the ROM.

The EROM can be erased by exposing it to high levels of ultraviolet light. This causes the insulating layer to temporarily break down, releasing the trapped charge. There are no large currents to introduce new current into this area and the ROM is erased. The EROM can now be reprogrammed as before. Note that the erasing and reprogramming is a very slow operation when compared with the writing of data in a random access memory. Thus, EROMs are only infrequently programmed. Note that the levels of ultraviolet light necessary to erase these ROMs is high so that exposure to ordinary room light does not erase them.

There are special microprocessor-controlled circuits that are used to program ROMs. In the more sophisticated ones, data can first be stored in the RAMs of these devices which then automatically program the ROM.

4-5. TAPE, DISK, AND DRUM MEMORIES

All of the memories that we have discussed thus far are random access memories, RAMs. In these memories, any memory address can be written into or read from without regard to any other memory address. As discussed, this is a very fast memory. We shall now talk about memories which are slower but provide much more storage at a lower price.

Actually, these slower forms of memory can store tremendous amounts of data. For instance, a bank may use them to store all of its depositors' records. Usually this is too much data to be stored in the main memory, but it can easily be stored on one or more magnetic tapes. When a program using this data is to be run, only the needed data is read from the tape into the main memory and then the program is executed. For instance, a single depositor's records can be read into the memory and processed. The resulting updated data is then recorded back on the tape. Next, another depositor's records are read into the main memory and the process is repeated. Thus, at any one time, only one depositor's records are stored in the main memory.

Programs can also be stored on tape. When they are to be used, they are read into the RAM. The slower storage techniques that we shall discuss in this section are very useful. Sometimes these slower storage techniques are used for the main memory. This slows the operation greatly, but it does provide a great deal of storage cheaply.

In most cases, these slower storage techniques store the data on *ferromagnetic* films, films which are made of magnetic material.

The operation differs from that of the main memory in that there is actual motion in this memory where the film moves in relation to a pick up device. In many respects, this is similar to an ordinary tape recorder where the magnetic tape moves in relation to the pickup or recording head.

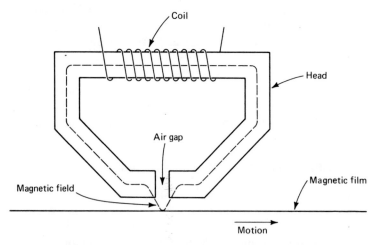

Fig. 4-11. An illustration of a magnetic film recording set up

The basic structure of this type of magnetic storage device is illustrated in Fig. 4-11. In all storage of this type, a thin layer of magnetic material is mounted on some support mechanism such as a tape or a disk and moved under a magnetic head. The head is made of ferromagnetic material and has a coil of wire wrapped around it. There is a small gap in the coil which is placed very close to the magnetic film. Note that the diagram of Fig. 4-11 is larger than an actual recorder head and it is not drawn to scale. The air gap is very small as is the spacing between the head and the magnetic film. When current is passed through the coil, a magnetic field is set up as shown. At the air gap, the magnetic field passes through the ferromagnetic film. This magnetizes the film. The magnetic film is moved under the head. If pulses of current are applied to the coil, then pulse-shaped regions will be magnetized on the film. In this way, information can be written on the film. Note that we can reverse the direction of the current which, in turn, reverses the polarity of the magnetic region.

Now suppose that there is no current in the coil and that the film is moved under the head. When a magnetized region passes under the head, a magnetic field will be set up in the ferromagnetic

Memories

head. When a non-magnetized region passes under the head, no magnetic field will be set up on the head. Thus, as the magnetic film moves under the head, the magnetism of the head will change. This changing magnetism will induce a voltage in the coil; information can now be read from the film by observing the voltage induced in the coil. (Note that there are usually separate heads used for the reading and writing of data.) There are several types of magnetic storage of this type. We shall now consider them.

Tape Recording

In one form of magnetic film storage, the magnetic film is supported by a thin plastic tape. This tape is wound on reels so that a very long tape can be easily stored or moved. Often there are many tracks on a tape, that is heads are usually positioned at different points along the width of the tape. Each of these tracks is used to store different information. This is analogous to an 8 track cassette recorder which stores 8 different channels of music. In the computer, some of the tracks store data. In addition, other tracks are used to provide the computer with such information as the position of the tape. Tapes often have information recorded at their beginning called a *directory*. This tells the computer where the data is stored on the tape. In general, tapes may store many different sets of data called *files*. For instance, one file may contain the account records of the customers of a store; another file may contain inventory information, etc. If you want to read a particular file, you must know its position on the tape. Suppose, for example, that a track can store 100,000 bits. Then, a particular file location might start at bit number 17,325. The track used to determine positions could contain a 1 for each bit position. Thus, by counting the number of 1's from the start of the tape, the computer can determine the bit numbers which define the position of that point on the tape that is under the head.

Tapes are written on and read from a *tape drive*. This contains the recording, play-back heads, and a mechanical drive system which turns the tape reels to move the tape under the heads. Tapes can be easily removed or inserted on the tape drive so that many different tapes can be used. Thus, the amount of information that can be stored on tapes is almost unlimited.

A single tape can store a great deal of information. For instance, a large tape which uses 6 heads for data storage can store 100 million bits. But the tape systems used with smaller computers are often much smaller; for example, the cassette system used with many personal computer stores less data. However, even these relatively small systems store large amounts of information and the cassettes can be easily changed so that many tapes can be used.

The amount of time that it takes for data to be read into or out of the memory is called the memory's *access time*. The primary disadvantage of tape memory is its large access time. An entire tape may have to be wound under the head before the desired data is obtained. Some tape drives can move the tape at very high speeds, for example 50 to 400 cm/sec. However, the access time is very long in comparison with other storage systems. Tape memories are called *sequential access* systems since the data is stored in sequence and we must move sequentially through the entire tape between the present location and the desired location to obtain any particular data.

Disk Memories

In the disk memory, the magnetic film is coated on a disk which resembles a phonograph record. Information is stored in tracks on the disk. These locations are concentric circles, *not* like the spiral track on ordinary phonograph records. The disk is rotated just as a phonograph record is except at a much higher speed. To read from or write on the disk, the head is positioned over the desired track. Then, to change tracks, the head must be moved radially.

Disk storage is much faster than tape storage since only a single track need be sequenced rather than all the data. Thus, on the average, the disk need only make one half a revolution before the desired data is positioned under the head. Thus, the access time of a disk is much shorter than that of a tape. The access time of the disk is slowed by the fact that the head must be moved from track to track, a precise operation which takes some time. To speed up the operation, there often are several heads on the disk drive. Thus, the average distance that any one head must move is less and the access time is reduced. A typical access time for a disk is 30 milliseconds; this is an average which includes the time for moving the heads from track to track. (This access time is much faster than a tape but very slow when compared with RAM.) Disk storage is not sequential access since we do not have to sequence through all the data as we do on a tape. On the other hand, it is not RAM. The terminology used for this type of memory is *direct access storage*.

Memories

There are two types of disk memories. One type, the original form which is used in most large computers, is called a *hard disk*. Normally enclosed in heavy plastic cases, these disks usually have a capacity for a million to 10 million bits.

Another form of disk is called the *floppy disk*. It is a thin disk stored in a heavy paper envelope. The fact that it is flexible gives it its name. The paper envelope has windows to provide access for the spindle that rotates the disk and for the heads. The disk is actually rotated within the paper envelope. In comparison with hard disks, floppy disks rotate at a slower rate and there is only one set of reading and writing heads. Thus, floppy disks have longer access times than hard disks. In addition, they do not store as much data as the hard disks, usually well under a million bits. Although they can be used very many times, the floppy disks also tend to wear out with use. If we want to use the floppy disk frequently, the information on it can be read into the RAM of the computer. This is then written on one or more floppy disks. Thus, backup disks are made and the fact that they wear out need not be a real problem. Note that all the information stored on a single floppy disk will usually be greater than the capacity of the RAM so that the transfer of data from one disk to another must be done in several steps.

The main advantage of floppy disks is that they are inexpensive. A single floppy disk costs only a few dollars. Consequently, large amounts of data can be easily and inexpensively stored. Note that, in most hard disk systems, disks can be taken off the disk drive and interchanged. Thus, disks as well as tapes can be used to store tremendous amounts of data. In general, hard disks are expensive so that this tends to limit somewhat the number of disks that are used.

Drum Memories

The fastest form of magnetic direct access memory is the drum memory. These memories were once used for main memories but have been supplanted by semiconductor and core memories. In a drum memory, the magnetic film is coated on a drum which is rapidly rotated. The data is again stored in tracks as it is on a disk. However, in a drum, there is a separate head for each track and this greatly reduces the access time.

Bubble Memories

A new form of magnetic memory that shows great promise is called the *bubble memory*. Small bubbles or regions of magnetic material are set up in a sheet of magnetic material. These can be read in sequential fashion. Bubble memories are nonvolatile and are slower than fast semiconductor memories. However, bubble memories can be used to provide relatively fast memories which store great amounts of data. For instance, 10 million bits can be stored in 6.5 cm^2 (1 sq in). Recent developments have enabled new bubble memories to be built that can store even more data in this small area. Bubble memories may possibly be used as the main memory in computers where it is desirable to sacrifice high speed in exchange for large amounts of storage. This is often true in the case of small computers.

4.6 CODES

The information stored in any memory word is a binary number, a sequence of 0's and 1's. In fact, all computer operations are designed in terms of binary numbers. Often, we want to store or work with data containing letters as well as numbers. For instance, a list of names can be stored and then alphabetized. Also, the program stored within the memory contains words. Data of this type is called *alphanumeric data*. In order to store alphanumeric data as sequences of 0's and 1's, *codes* are used. (A code is a certain sequence of binary numbers that represent letters and symbols.) The computer must be programmed to process this data properly. For example, a terminal is wired so that it types a certain letter or number in response to a sequence of 0's and 1's. When the program requires that certain words be typed, the computer must send the correct sequence of symbols to the terminal.

Let us consider two codes that are commonly used in computers: the ASCII (American Standard Code for Information Interchange) and the EBCDIC (Extended Binary Coded Decimal Interchange Code).

Note that there are codes for numbers as well as for letters. For instance, when we transmit data from a Teletype to a computer, these codes are used for the numbers. They are then converted within the computer to their binary representations. In general, in such data transmission, it is convenient for all symbols to be represented by sequences of 0's and 1's which are of equal lengths. We have also given the codes for some symbols such as +, -, * and

SOME ALPHANUMERIC CODES

	ASCII code	EBCDIC code
A	100 0001	1100 0001
B	100 0010	1100 0010
C	100 0011	1100 0011
D	100 0100	1100 0100
E	100 0101	1100 0101
F	100 0110	1100 0110
G	100 0111	1100 0111
H	100 1000	1100 1000
I	100 1001	1100 1001
J	100 1010	1101 0001
K	100 1011	1101 0010
L	100 1100	1101 0011
M	100 1101	1101 0100
N	100 1110	1101 0101
O	100 1111	1101 0110
P	101 0000	1101 0111
Q	101 0001	1101 1000
R	101 0010	1101 1001
S	101 0011	1110 0010
T	101 0100	1110 0011
U	101 0101	1110 0100
V	101 0110	1110 0101
W	101 0111	1110 0110
X	101 1000	1110 0111
Y	101 1001	1110 1000
Z	101 1010	1110 1001
0	011 0000	1111 0000
1	011 0001	1111 0001
2	011 0010	1111 0010
3	011 0011	1111 0011
4	011 0100	1111 0100
5	011 0101	1111 0101
6	011 0110	1111 0110
7	011 0111	1111 0111
8	011 1000	1111 1000
9	011 1001	1111 1001
blank	000 0000	0100 0000
.	010 1110	0100 1011

(	010 1000	0100 1101
+	010 1011	0100 1110
}	101 1101	0100 1111
{	101 1011	0101 1010
$	010 0100	0101 1011
*	010 1010	0101 1100
)	010 1001	0101 1101
;	011 1011	0101 1110
,	010 1100	0110 1011
-	010 1101	0110 1101
=	011 1101	0111 1110

$ here. While actually there is provision made for more symbols, we have only included the common ones in this table.

Note that these codes are arranged in numerical order; the binary value of the code representation of an A is less than that for a B. This is useful in computer programs that alphabetize lists. We have only shown capital letters in our list. The codes also provide for lowercase letters. Notice that the three leftmost bits in the ASCII for capital letters are 100 for A to O and 101 for P to Z. If the 100 is replaced by 110 and the 101 is replaced by 111, the ASCII code for lowercase letters results. In EBCDIC, a similar change occurs. Now the first four digits are changed to obtain lowercase letters. In particular, 1100 is replaced by 1000, 1101 is replaced by 1001, and 1110 is replaced by 1010.

Error Detecting Codes

The input to a computer is often sent over telephone lines where noise may affect the signal and make a 0 appear as a 1 or vice versa. Some codes are designed so that an error in a single bit can be detected. One such code is called a *parity check* code. Here, an extra bit called a *parity bit* is added to the code. The bit is either a 0 or a 1 and is constructed so that the total number of 1's in the coded representation of a letter or number is even. Each time that the sequence representing a symbol is received, the computer makes a check. If the total number of 1's is not even, then the symbol is rejected and an error message is sent, calling for the retransmission of the correct symbol. We have illustrated a parity check code with an even number of bits, but sometimes an odd number of bits is used. These error checking codes are *not* always used.

Memories

EXERCISES

4-1. Discuss the organization of a memory.

4-2. What is meant by the address of a word?

4-3. Discuss the operation of the memory cell in Fig. 4-1b for all inputs and control signals.

4-4. Describe the operation of the memory in Fig. 4-2 in your own words.

4-5. Draw an 8 word four-bit semiconductor memory.

4-6. Discuss how material is erased from the memory in Fig. 4-2.

4-7. Discuss the operation of the decoder in Fig. 4-3.

4-8. Draw a memory decoder that inputs a three-bit binary number and drives eight internal address lines.

4-9. Describe the operation of the memory in Fig. 4-4 in your own words.

4-10. Discuss the reasons for paralleling memory chips.

4-11. Modify the decoder you designed in Exercise 4-8 so that it has a chip select line.

4-12. Discuss the function of the output enable line.

4-13. Show how a 32 word, four-bit memory can be constructed by paralleling a sufficient number of 8 word, four-bit chips.

4-14. Discuss the operation of a magnetic core.

4-15. Discuss the reading of a magnetic core.

4-16. Discuss the operation of ROMs. In particular, consider the input and output signals.

4-17. Discuss and compare the ordinary ROM, the PROM, and the erasable ROM.

4-18. Discuss and compare tape, disk, and drum storages.

4-19. What is the difference between a hard disk and a floppy disk?

4-20. What are the differences among random access, sequential access, and direct access storage systems?

4-21. Discuss the need for alphanumeric codes.

4-22. Write the word BOOK in ASCII code.

4-23. Discuss parity checking codes.

5 Basic Digital Computation

In this chapter we shall discuss the way in which computations are performed in a digital computer. We shall discuss the details of how numbers are added and multiplied. We shall also consider some other important operations. Since these computations are done in the binary number system, we shall discuss operations in binary to see how these relate to the digital computer.

5-1. THE BASIC ARITHMETIC LOGIC UNIT—MODULAR ARITHMETIC

In a computer, the basic arithmetic operations are performed in the arithmetic logic unit—ALU. This contains one or more registers called *accumulators*, where results of calculations are stored. For the sake of simplicity, let us assume that the ALU contains only one accumulator. (Note that although the notation used here is fairly standard, the word accumulator is, at times, used to refer to the complete ALU.)

A typical arithmetic operation would consist of the following: A number is read from the memory and input to the ALU where it is added to the number already stored in the accumulator. This result becomes the final number stored in the accumulator. The ALU can do more than store and add numbers. In this section we shall concentrate on these two features but others will be considered later.

In Sec. 3-4 we considered the full adder, the gate circuit for which was shown in Fig. 3-17. We shall use this full adder as a part of the ALU. Let us represent the full adder by the block diagram

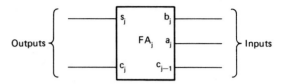

Fig. 5-1. The block diagram of a full adder

in Fig. 5-1. This adder adds three single bit binary numbers b_j, a_j, and c_{j-1}, to obtain the sum s_j and c_j. Remember that in Sec. 3-4 we said that b_j and a_j represent the jth bits in the number and that c_{j-1} is the carry from the j-1st column. To illustrate this, the three-bit adder which adds the following two binary numbers is shown in Fig. 5-2.

$$b_2 b_1 b_0$$
$$+ a_2 a_1 a_0$$

The resulting sum is the binary number:

$$s_2 s_1 s_0$$

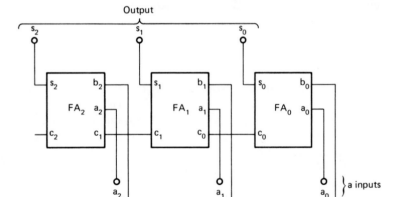

Fig. 5-2. A three bit adder

Note that c_2, the carry out of the leftmost column, is not used. If the sum is a four-bit number, then an overflow results. This was discussed in Sec. 2-3. The c_2 output can be used to indicate if an overflow has occurred. If $c_2 = 1$, then an overflow has occurred. This signal (c_2) could be used to cause a warning message to be typed out on your terminal.

Basic Digital Computation

Now let us combine this adder with a simple parallel input-parallel output register to form a very simple ALU. Such a register was discussed in Sec. 3-8. (Note that the circuit in Fig. 3-30 functions as a parallel input-parallel output register when the control signals are $c_0 = c_1 = 0$, $c_2 = 1$, $c_3 = 0$.) Note that in the ALU (Fig. 5-3) we could have used a more complex register such as the one illustrated in Fig. 3-30, but we avoided this in order to keep the circuit simple.

In the operation of Fig. 5-3, there are two control lines, ADD and CLEAR. If we want to ADD, then a 1 signal is placed on the ADD line and a 0 on the CLEAR. Now suppose that a number is stored in the accumulator and ADD = 1 and CLEAR = 0. The output of each flip-flop is connected to the a input of the corresponding full adder; the number stored in the accumulator will be one of the numbers to be added. The other number to be added is applied to the b input terminals of the full adder. After the addition is complete, the sum of the two numbers will be $s_2 s_1 s_0$.

Now let us see how this sum is stored in the accumulator. Since CLEAR = 0, one input to each of AND gates e_2, e_1, and e_0 will be 1. Hence,

$$D_0 = s_0 \qquad (5\text{-}1a)$$

$$D_1 = s_1 \qquad (5\text{-}1b)$$

$$D_2 = s_2 \qquad (5\text{-}1c)$$

Then, *after* the next clock pulse, the number stored in the accumulator will be the desired sum. Note that master-slave or edge-triggered flip-flops are used. Hence, the output does not change until *after* the clock pulse. Thus, if a number is stored in the accumulator, that number will remain there until after the next clock pulse. Assume that the number to be added appears at the output of the flip-flops after a clock pulse which we (arbitrarily) number 1. During the time that the clock pulse is off (between clock pulse number 1 and clock pulse number 2) the addition takes place. Then, at the next clock pulse (clock pulse number 2) the input to the flip-flops will be the new sum. The output of the flip-flops have not yet changed. Thus, the a_2, a_1, and a_0 inputs to the adder do not change until after clock pulse 2. The internal states of the flip-flops have already changed to the desired sum. Hence, after clock pulse 2, the output of the flip-flop becomes the desired number. Note that all this assumes that the adders are fast enough (or that the clock pulses are far enough apart) so that the addition can take place in the time between clock pulses.

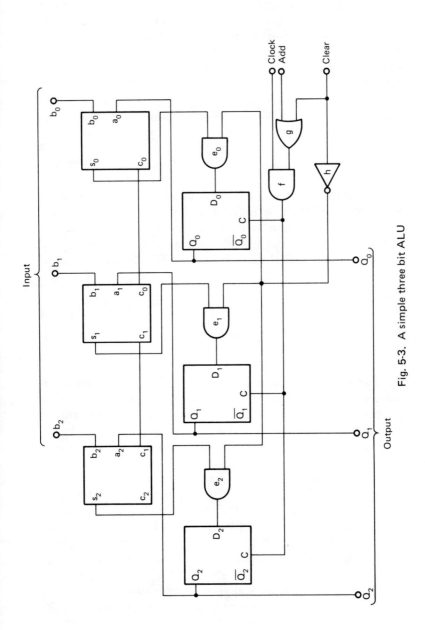

Fig. 5-3. A simple three bit ALU

Basic Digital Computation

If both ADD = 0 and CLEAR = 0, then no clock pulse or input signal is applied to the flip-flops, and the number stored in the accumulator remains there. If ADD = 0 and CLEAR = 1, then all inputs to the flip-flops will be 0, since the lower input to AND gates e_0, e_1, and e_2 are now 0. Then, at the next clock pulse, the accumulator will set itself to 0. Thus, the accumulator has been cleared. One fact should be noted. The input number $b_2 b_1 b_0$ is usually stored in a register. This register can be part of the ALU or external to it. If it is internal, then the ALU will have two registers, which are both often called accumulators. We have not shown such a second register here in order to keep the diagram simple.

5-2. MODULAR ARITHMETIC

ALU addition is different from addition done by hand. Since the register in an ALU can only store a fixed number of bits, overflow can result. It may seem as though this property of the ALU is totally disadvantageous, but we shall see how it can be put to use in this and the next section.

First we shall familiarize ourselves with some of the details of number storage, working with a base 10 accumulator. The ordinary automobile odometer serves as a useful example. Let us assume that we have one which goes up to 99 miles and then resets to 0. (We use the number 99 rather than 99999 to keep the numbers smaller.) Then, the odometer's readings will be:

$$\begin{array}{c} 00 \\ 01 \\ 02 \\ \cdot \\ \cdot \\ \cdot \\ 10 \\ 11 \\ 12 \\ \cdot \\ \cdot \\ \cdot \\ 96 \\ 97 \\ 98 \\ 99 \end{array}$$

00
01
02
.
.
.

The accumulator can store numbers from 0 to 99. If we add additional numbers then it cycles again. Accumulators in computers also function in this way. Now, suppose that the odometer reads 26. We are not sure if the car has been driven 26 miles or any of the following distances:

$$26 \\ 126 \\ 226 \qquad (5\text{-}2)$$

.
.
.

(Keep in mind that there could also be negative numbers. This case will be considered in the next section.)

If we are dealing with a register that can store numbers up to 99, then the numbers 26, 126, 226, ..., all lead to equivalent readings. Similarly, 47, 147, 247, 347, ..., are equivalent. Let us now introduce a notation that takes this into account. The symbol $\equiv_{100}$ will be used here. For instance, we can write:

$$26 \equiv_{100} 126 \equiv_{100} 226 \qquad (5\text{-}3)$$

The symbol $\equiv_{100}$ indicates that the equivalence is for a register that stores 100 numbers (0, 1, ..., 99). We read it as *equivalent, modulo* 100 or *congruent, modulo* 100. That is, 26 and 126 are equivalent, modulo 100. Again, this means that each of these will result in the *same* output of the register.

If we want to find the numbers that are equivalent, modulo 100, to a given number, then we add 100 to it. For instance, 26, 26 + 100, 26 + 200, etc. are all equivalent, modulo 100.

There is essentially no difference if we use a binary register. For example, let us use a three-bit accumulator. If we keep adding 1 to it, we have:

000
001
010
011
100

$$\begin{array}{l}101\\110\\111\\000\\001\\010\\011\\100\\\cdot\\\cdot\\\cdot\end{array} \qquad (5\text{-}4)$$

As an example, suppose that the register reads 011_2. We are not sure how many times the register has been cycled, so that 011_2 could represent 3_{10}, 11_{10}, or 19_{10}. Then, using the previous notation, we could say:

$$3 \equiv_8 11 \equiv_8 19 \qquad (5\text{-}5)$$

Similarly, if we choose a different example:

$$4 \equiv_8 12 \equiv_8 20 \equiv_8 28 \qquad (5\text{-}6)$$

Let us look at this in a somewhat different way. Suppose that we have a three-bit register. Then, if we add 8_{10} to the number, we will cycle it through 8 steps and come back to our *starting point*. Similarly, if we have a four-bit accumulator and we add 16 to the number stored in its register, there will be *no change* in the stored number. While it may seem as though this would not lead to any practical results, in the next section we shall show how these ideas can be used to simplify computer circuits.

Before considering any further details of modular arithmetic, let us discuss subtraction in binary. Suppose that we subtract the following:

$$\begin{array}{rcl}1011 & \leftarrow & \text{minuend}\\-0110 & \leftarrow & \text{subtrahend}\\\hline 0101 & \leftarrow & \text{difference}\end{array}$$

Normally, we subtract column by column. However, the bit in the third column of the subtrahend is larger than that of the minuend; thus we must "borrow" from the fourth column. The subtraction operation could then be written as:

$$\begin{array}{r}0\ 10\ 1\ 1\\-0\ \ \ 1\ 1\ 0\\\hline 0\ \ \ 1\ 0\ 1\end{array}$$

We have borrowed 8_{10} from the fourth column and added it to the third column.

Now consider another subtraction:

$$\begin{array}{r} 0110 \\ -1011 \\ \hline -0101 \end{array}$$

Since the number that we are subtracting (the subtrahend) is larger than the minuend, the answer is negative. The procedure for indicating negative numbers is considered in the next section.

5-3. 2'S COMPLEMENT ARITHMETIC

In Sec. 5-1 we discussed the circuit of an ALU that could be used to perform addition. Full adders were used to actually add the bits. If we want to perform subtraction, we could build a logic circuit that performs that function; analogous to a full adder, we could build a full subtractor. In many cases this is not done since it means that we would need additional computer circuits or *hardware*. This would increase the size and cost of the computer. (It would, however, also increase its speed, which is an advantage.) We shall now show that by taking the modular properties of the ALU into account, we can perform subtraction using the basic modular adder (one that adds). Thus, we shall not have to add additional hardware in order to perform subtraction. In addition, we shall see that this procedure will let us work with negative numbers conveniently.

To see how we can perform subtraction without using a subtractor circuit, suppose that we are working with a four-bit register and that we wnat to subtract 4 from 9. We shall first write the number in base 10 and then repeat the operations in binary. Thus, we have:

$$9 - 4 = 5$$

Now suppose that we add 16 to the number stored in the register. As discussed in the last section, the register will cycle completely and there will be *no change* in the stored number. Thus, we can write:

$$16 + 9 - 4 = 5 + 16 \equiv_{16} 5 \qquad (5\text{-}7)$$

Now let us rewrite the left hand side of the equation as:

$$15 + 1 + 9 - 4 = (15 - 4) + 1 + 9 \qquad (5\text{-}8)$$

Basic Digital Computation

To perform the operation, we subtract 4 from 15 and then add one and then add nine. Remember that we are trying to avoid building subtractor circuits. It may seem as though we have accomplished nothing here since we still have to subtract 4 from 15. However, when we do this in binary, the operation is quite simple. Fifteen is the largest number that can be stored in a four bit register:

$$15_{10} = 1111_2$$

This number is all 1's. Now consider subtraction from such a number. In binary, $15 - 4$ is:

$$\begin{array}{r} 1111 \\ -\,0100 \\ \hline 1011 \end{array}$$

Note that the result can be obtained directly from the subtrahend, 0100, simply by complementing each of its bits. If we subtract any four bit subtrahend from 1111_2, the difference is obtained simply by complementing *each* bit of the subrahend. This complementing operation requires no additional hardware. In general, all numbers to be processed are stored in registers containing flip-flops. For instance, suppose that a number is stored in the accumulator in Fig. 5-3. If we want to complement its bits, we need only take the output at $\bar{Q}_2$, $\bar{Q}_1$, and $\bar{Q}_0$. This number is always available and no additional hardware is needed.

Now we perform the subtraction of 4 from 9 in binary. Using this procedure, $4 = 0100_2$. First we reverse all the bits to get 1011. Then add $1_{10} = 0001_2$. Next, add $9_{10} = 1011_2$. Hence:

$$\begin{array}{r} 1011 \\ +\,0001 \\ +\,1001 \\ \hline 10101 \end{array}$$

Note the leftmost bit. This will not appear in the four-bit register. The register will only contain:

$$0101_2 = 5_{10}$$

This yields the correct answer. If we did not work with registers, then adding $15 + 1 = 16$ would give an answer that was too large by the amount 16. However, adding 16 in a register just cycles the four-bit register back to where it started, since the leftmost (fifth) bit is lost. Hence, we have used the modular arithmetic properties to advantage.

Here is another example. Suppose that we subtract 7 from 12. Then, $7_{10} = 0111$. Reversing each bit yields 1000. Then, we add 0001 and $12_{10} = 1100_2$ to obtain the correct result.

$$\begin{array}{r} 1000 \\ 0001 \\ \underline{1100} \\ 10101 \end{array}$$

Discarding the leftmost bit, we have $0101_2 = 5_{10}$, which is the correct answer. Let us write this in general terms. Suppose that we have a register and that the largest number that it can store is $R - 1$. For instance, if we have a four-bit register, then $R - 1 = 15$. Using this system, assume that we want to perform the subtraction:

$$D = A - B \tag{5-9}$$

We actually perform:

$$(R - 1) - B + 1 + A \tag{5-10}$$

Remember that $(R - 1) - B$ is easy to perform since it only involves complementing each bit of B. The remaining additions then give the correct result. Hence, we only need adders, not subtractors, to perform subtraction.

The 2's Complement

The name given to the operation that we have just discussed is taking the *2's complement* of a number N. It is defined in the following way:

$$C_2 = 2^k - N \tag{5-11}$$

where k is the number of bits in the register. For instance, if we have a four-bit register $2^4 = 16$, the 2's complement of $4_{10} = 0100_2$ is:

$$C_2 = 16_{10} - 4_{10} = 12_{10}$$

Note that when we took $(R - 1) - B + 1$ in Eq. (5-10), we were actually taking the 2's complement of B. From the previous discussion we see that it is easy to take the 2's complement; we need only replace all the bits of the number by their complements and then add 1. Hence, if we are working with four bits, the 2's complement of $0101_2 = 5_{10}$ is:

$$\begin{array}{r} 1010 \\ + 0001 \\ \hline 1011 \end{array}$$

Basic Digital Computation

As we have shown, the number stored in a register is a binary representation of a decimal number. However, we can look at it in a different way. The sequence of bits, which we call a binary number, could be a code that represents a decimal number. We could arrange this code so that the binary number did not equal its decimal equivalent. We could still build gate circuits that would add these numbers and give the correct results when they were converted back to decimal; but this code would be an unnecessary complication and the logic circuits would be unduly complicated. Hence, we do not do it for positive numbers. However, when we deal with negative numbers, we must use some sort of code since registers only store 0's and 1's and not minus signs.

Of the many codes that can be employed, we shall discuss one that is widely used and that makes computation simple. It does this because the results are correct in terms of modular arithmetic. The 2's complement can be used to obtain such a procedure. Suppose that we have a four-bit register. The numbers that it stores are:

$$
\begin{array}{l}
\vdots\\
1011\\
1100\\
1101\\
1110\\
1111 \quad \leftarrow 2_{10} - 3_{10} = -1_{10}\\
0000\\
0001 \hspace{4em} (5\text{-}12)\\
0010 \quad \leftarrow 2_{10}\\
0011\\
0100\\
0101 \quad \leftarrow 5_{10} = 2_{10} + 3_{10}\\
0110\\
0111\\
1000\\
\vdots
\end{array}
$$

Now suppose that we add 3_{10} to a number. This means that we move forward (down) 3 positions in the register. This is shown in (5-12), where we have added 3_{10} to 2_{10}. Now suppose that we subtract 3_{10}. This is equivalent to moving backwards (up) 3 positions in the register. If we cycle backwards 16 positions in the four-bit register, we will return to our original starting position. Thus, if a register reads $0100_2 = 4_{10}$, we do not know if it represents 4 or 4 + 16 = 20, or 4 + 32 = 36, or 4 − 16 = −12, or 4 − 32 = −28 and so on. In (5-12), the result of $2_{10} - 3_{10}$ is $1111_2 = 15_{10}$. However, we can now write:

$$15 \equiv_{16} -1 \qquad (5\text{-}13)$$

That is, 15 is equivalent, modulo 16 to −1.

Now if we define 1111 to be −1 in our code, the correct answer would be obtained. Similarly, 1110 would represent −2. Suppose that we want to use four bits to represent numbers between −7 and +7. We can use the following table:

Table 5-1: Four-bit binary representation of numbers from −7 to +7 using 2's complement for negative numbers

Decimal number	Binary number
−7	1001
−6	1010
−5	1011
−4	1100
−3	1101
−2	1110
−1	1111
0	0000
1	0001
2	0010
3	0011
4	0100
5	0101
6	0110
7	0111

This table is consistent with our previous discussion. But the negative numbers are now simply the 2's complement of their positive equivalents. For example, to obtain the representation of −7, we take $7_{10} = 0111_2$ and take its 2's complement. This is:

$$\begin{array}{r} 1000 \\ +\ 0001 \\ \hline 1001 \end{array}$$

Similarly, we can obtain all of the other negative numbers in the table. If the leftmost digit is 0, the number is positive, while if the

Basic Digital Computation

leftmost digit is 1, the number is negative. *Note that we do not make a number negative simply by replacing the leftmost 0 with a 1.*

If we have b bits in a register, we now only use b − 1 of them to represent the size of the number. For instance, in Table 5-1, we have four bits, but the numbers only range between −7 and +7. If we worked with positive numbers only, then the numbers would range between 0 and 15_{10}.

Use of 2's Complement in Subtraction

Using a four-bit system and working with subtraction, we shall now show that the use of the 2's complement to represent negative numbers actually works. Suppose that we want to subtract 4 from 7. This is equivalent to adding 7 to −4. Then, $7_{10} = 0111_2$ and $4_{10} = 0100_2$. Taking the 2's complement of 4, we obtain 1100. Then, adding this to 0111, we have:

$$\begin{array}{r} 0111 \\ + 1100 \\ \hline 10011 \end{array}$$

Ignoring the leftmost digit, we have $0011_2 = 3_{10}$, which is the correct answer to 7 − 4. Again, note that we have used the properties of modular arithmetic to obtain the correct result. Consider another example. Subtract 6 from 3. Then, the 2's complement of 6 is 1010, (Table 5-1). Hence, to obtain 3 minus 6 we take:

$$\begin{array}{r} 0011 \\ + 1010 \\ \hline 1101 \end{array}$$

Using Table 5-1, note that $1101_2 = -3$, which is the correct answer.

Let us clarify one thing. In some of the previous examples, we ignore overflow by throwing away the (fifth) leftmost bit. Actually, this is *not* an example of *true overflow*. The only time that a true overflow occurs is when the size of the resulting number is too large. For instance, if we add $7_{10} + 5_{10}$, we have:

$$\begin{array}{r} 0111 \\ + 0101 \\ \hline 1100 \end{array}$$

The answer is 1100_2, which, according to the table, is −4. The actual answer should be 12. Hence, a true overflow has occurred and we get the *wrong* answer. For a four-bit system, a true overflow occurs when the magnitude of the answer is greater than 7. Similarly, in a k-bit system, a true overflow occurs when the magnitude of the answer exceeds $2^{k-1} - 1$.

5-4. MULTIPLICATION AND DIVISION

Let us now see what is involved when multiplication or division is performed on a computer. We begin by discussing what we would do if we multiplied two binary numbers using pencil and paper. The rules for multiplication in binary follow those for multiplication of decimal numbers. However, we shall see that the use of binary tends to simplify the operation. Suppose that we multiply 1101 by 1011:

1101	multiplicand	
1011	multiplier	
1101	first partial product	
1101	second partial product	(5-14)
0000	third partial product	
1101	fourth partial product	
10001111	product	

We multiply the multiplicand by the rightmost digit (1) to obtain the first partial product. Next, we multiply the multiplicand by the second digit (1) of the multiplier, shift the resulting partial product one digit to the left and add the result to the first partial product. Next, we multiply the multiplicand by the third digit of the multiplier (0) and shift the partial product two digits to the right and add the result to the previous sum of partial products. This process is repeated with all the digits of the multiplier.

Multiplication in binary is easier than the corresponding multiplication in decimal, since the partial products in binary are obtained by multiplying either by 1 or by 0. When multiplication is done in decimal, we may have to multiply by any of the digits from 0 to 9.

Let us see how this process can be implemented in a digital computer. Note that the product of two four-bit numbers is an eight-bit number. Since most small computers work with eight-bit numbers, we shall assume that we are working with eight-bit numbers here. That is, we can consider the multiplicand and multiplier to be 00001011 and 00001101, respectively. Notice that the multiplier and multiplicand must be small enough so that the product does not require more than eight bits. This is true in the case we are discussing. Now suppose that we have both the multiplier and the multiplicand stored in two shift registers. First we

Basic Digital Computation

examine the rightmost bit of the multiplier's shift register. If it is a 1, then the multiplicand is input to an ALU and added. If the rightmost bit of the multiplicand is a 0, then the multiplier's shift register contents are not added to the contents of the accumulator. We can achieve this operation by having the rightmost bit of the multiplier shift register output connected to the ADD control of the ALU (Fig. 5-3) so that the addition takes place when the rightmost bit stored in the multiplier shift register is a 1.

Now the contents of the multiplicand's shift register are shifted one unit to the left. Thus, it is in position to add the second partial product. The multiplier's shift register is shifted to the right, causing the original rightmost bit of the multiplier to be lost. The bit occupying the rightmost position of the multiplier's shift register is now the second bit of the multiplier. Remember that this bit controls the ADD operation. If this bit is a 1, then the contents of the multiplicand shift register (which has been shifted to the left) are added to the accumulator. If the new rightmost bit in the multiplier shift register is a 0, then no addition takes place.

The shift registers are shifted again. The process then repeats itself for each bit of the multiplier. When the process is complete, the contents of the accumulator will be the desired product.

Some computers have circuits whose function is to perform multiplication. The circuit contains registers and accumulators, as we have just discussed, so that when two numbers are supplied, their product is produced. A circuit of this type is called a *hard wired multiplier*. Not all hard wired multipliers function as we have discussed. Sometimes circuit simplifications are used, but the basic ideas are the same as those presented in this discussion. If a simple computer does not contain a hard wired multiplier, it must be programmed with step by step instructions to perform multiplication. In the next chapter we shall discuss such programming which is often tedious, involving many steps. But if there is hard wiring, then only one command need be given to obtain multiplication; the computer circuitry, however, is more complex when hard wiring is used.

Let us now see how a computer performs division. Just as multiplication involves addition, division involves subtraction. Suppose that we divide 10001111 by 1011. (This is the inverse of the multiplication in Eq. (5-14).) The first step would be to see if 1011 is greater than 1000. Since it is, we would not attempt the first step in the division. But the computer is not aware of this and would perform the following division:

```
      1011 ⟌ 10001111
             −1011
```

After the subtraction is performed, the result is tested to see if it is negative. (We shall discuss a circuit that tests for negative numbers in Sec. 5-6.) If it is, then this step in the division should not be performed. The computer is programmed so that all of the previous operations are ignored. Thus, in this case, the following is attempted next:

```
                 01
      1011 ⟌ 10001111
             − 1011
               0110111
```

(Actually, the subtraction would be done using 2's complement as discussed in the last section.) The procedure would be repeated until the quotient 01101 was obtained.

Computers either can be built with hard wired dividers or they can be programmed to divide numbers. The latter case results in simpler computer circuitry but requires much more tedious programming. We shall discuss such a program as well as procedures for simplifying it in the next chapter.

5-5. FLOATING POINT NUMBERS

Often, especially in engineering or scientific calculations, we deal with very large or very small numbers. To avoid writing large numbers of digits, we express these numbers in terms of a number with fewer digits which is multiplied by 10 raised to some power. The power is an integer (whole number). For example, the following representations are equivalent:

$$1,763,000 = .1763 \times 10^7 \qquad (5\text{-}15)$$

Similarly:

$$0.0000000112304 = .112304 \times 10^{-7} \qquad (5\text{-}16)$$

In a computer, this is called *floating point notation*, since changing the exponent effectively allows the position of the decimal point to "float" or vary. Let us define the terms used in Eqs.(5-15) and (5-16). For instance, in Eq. (5-15), the 7 is called the *exponent*, while 0.1763 is called the *fractional part*. Another widely used name for the fractional part is the *mantissa*. Actually, this name is misleading since it is *not* the mantissa of the logarithm of a number, so we shall use the term "fractional part."

When floating point numbers are used in digital computers, we usually work with powers of 2 rather than with powers of 10. For instance, $64_{10} = 2^7$ can be written as:

$$0.1 \times (10_2)^{1000_2}$$

It is more convenient, of course, to write this as:

$$0.1_2 \times 2^8$$

the fractional part given in binary, the exponent in decimal. (But remember that the computer only works in binary.)

Let us clarify a point that sometimes causes confusion. There is a difference between number size and the number of significant figures. For instance, suppose that we express a length in millionths of a centimeter as 1,736,000. Although the actual length may be 1,736,401, we cannot measure it accurately enough to ascertain this. In this case, we say that we know the number (1,736,000) to four significant figures.

When we work with numbers in floating point form, we actually work with two numbers, the fractional part and the exponent. Each of these must be stored. Often, they are stored in the same register. For instance, if the register stores twelve bits, the eight leftmost bits may be used to store the fractional part and the four rightmost bits used to store the exponent.

Suppose that we have the number:

$$.00010110111 \times 2^{-6} = .10110111 \times 2^{-9} \qquad (5\text{-}17)$$

It would require eleven bits to store the fractional part of the left-hand side of Eq. (5-17) while it only requires eight bits to store the fractional part of the right-hand side of the equation. Yet, they are the same number. If the fractional part is stored in eight bits of the register, then the left-hand side representation of Eq. (5-17) would result in .00010110's being stored. This represents a loss of significant figures and, hence, a loss of accuracy. To avoid this, the exponents of floating point numbers stored in computers are adjusted so that the bit immediately to the right of the binary point is a 1. Such numbers are said to have been *normalized* or *scaled*. In this case, storage space is not wasted on zeros. Note that the binary point is *not* stored. For instance, in Eq. (5-17), the stored fractional part would be 10110111. In scaled floating point, the location of the binary point is just to the left of the number, and thus there is no need to store it.

With regard to signs, both the fractional part and the exponent can be either positive or negative. Thus, there must be provision for sign bits here: one bit is used to store the sign of the exponent and one is used to store the sign of the fractional part. (The 2's complement discussion in Sec. 5-3 provides a procedure for indicating negative numbers.)

In order to see what size numbers the computer can work with, let us talk about storage. A register will store a given number of bits. Groups of bits are called *bytes*. Typically, a group of eight bits is called a *byte*. Usually, most registers in a computer are the same length. We call this length the *word size* of the computer. A typical word size could be two (8 bit) bytes or 16 bits.

Now let us see how large or small the stored number can be. Assume that the word length is 32 bits. This must store both the exponential and fractional parts and their signs. Two of the 32 bits will be used to store the signs, leaving 30 bits. Usually, 6 of these are used to store the magnitude of the exponent and the other 24 are used to store the fractional part. Now the largest number that can be stored for the exponent is:

$$2^6 - 1 = 63_{10}$$

Then:

$$2^{63} = 9.223 \times 10^{18} \qquad (5\text{-}18)$$

This is a very large number. Similarly, 2^{-63} is a very small number. Hence, we can express very large and very small numbers using this procedure.

We have assumed that the exponent raises two to a power. Actually, it could be a power of some other number. For instance, in some computers, it is a power of 16; the appropriate logic circuits are arranged to account for this. Now, if we have 6 bits in which to store the magnitude of the exponent, we still have the same number, 63_{10}, for the exponent. Now, however, it raises 16_{10} to a power. Thus, the exponential part can be as large as:

$$16^{63} = 7.237 \times 10^{75} \qquad (5\text{-}19)$$

This is much larger than the number given in (5-18).

Now let us talk about the fractional part which we have stored in 24 bits. For example, a number stored might be:

.101100111100110010110011

The more places that we store, the more accuracy we have. Suppose that we only store 23 bits. The last bit to the right would be lost. This bit represents:

$$2^{-24} = .0000000596_{10}$$

But, if there were only 23 bits in the fractional part, we would lose this number. For example, if we have the numbers $.12461281_{10}$ and $.12461282_{10}$, both of them would be stored as the same number. Note that there are seven significant figures here because there are seven zeros to the right of the decimal point in the decimal representation of 2^{-24}.

These numbers are actually quite accurate. In most engineering and scientific applications, we cannot measure data this accurately. On the other hand, we often lose accuracy when we perform calculations. For example, when we multiply two eight-bit fractional parts, we end up with a sixteen-bit fractional part. If we throw away the 8 rightmost bits, accuracy is lost. Certain computer programs require many calculations, and if we lose a little accuracy with each computation, the final result may be greatly in error. Thus, we often need great precision when complex computations are performed, and at times, seven or eight significant figures are insufficient. Most computers, however, can be programmed so that two or more registers or memory locations are used to store a single number, thus providing additional precision. This operation is usually called *double precision*.

We have considered a word with 32 bits. Most small computers have smaller words, usually 8 or 16 bits in length. Although it may appear that these computers cannot be used for calculations, this is *not* the case. For one thing, many programs perform numerical calculations that do not require many significant figures or large numbers. In such cases, we do not require a large number of bits to store the fractional part and the exponent. In addition, there are many programs that do not do numerical calculations. For example, programs may alphabetize lists of names, keep track of inventory, play games, or control the operation of an alarm system. In such cases, since large numbers with many digits are *not* used at all, small word-length computers can be used for all these applications. And provided it is properly programmed, a small word-length computer can also be used for engineering or scientific computations. As we discussed above, we may use several registers or memory locations to store a single number; for instance, instead of storing a number in a single memory location, we can store it in two. Of course, this effectively means that there is less memory. However, there is usually sufficient memory to perform the desired calculations.

Addition and Subtraction

When we add or subtract floating point numbers, the exponents must be the same. For instance, if we want to add $.1001 \times 2^8$ and $.1011 \times 2^7$, we would write:

$$\begin{array}{r} .1001 \times 2^8 \\ +\ .01011 \times 2^8 \\ \hline .11101 \times 2^8 \end{array}$$

If we only store four bits for the fractional part, there is going to be some loss of accuracy since, instead of storing the answer $.11101 \times 2^8$, we are storing $.1110 \times 2^8$. This is called *roundoff error*. Often, these errors are small enough to be ignored. When greater accuracy is desired, however, *double precision* must be employed.

Multiplication and Division

When we multiply and divide floating point numbers, we use the ordinary rules for multiplication and division of numbers with exponents. Suppose that we have two numbers:

$$A = F_a 2^{E_a} \qquad (5\text{-}20\text{a})$$

$$B = F_b 2^{E_b} \qquad (5\text{-}20\text{b})$$

where F_a and F_b are the fractional parts, and E_a and E_b are the exponents. To multiply the numbers, we multiply their fractional parts and add their exponents. Thus:

$$A \times B = F_a F_b 2^{E_a + E_b} \qquad (5\text{-}21)$$

For instance, suppose that:

$$A = .1011 \times 2^5 \qquad (5\text{-}22\text{a})$$

$$B = .1101 \times 2^7 \qquad (5\text{-}22\text{b})$$

Then:

$$A \times B = .010001111 \times 2^{12}$$

In a computer, this would usually be scaled and stored as:

$$A \times B = 0.10001111 \times 2^{11}$$

Note that there are more digits in the fractional part of the product than in either A or B, meaning that roundoff error can occur here also.

Basic Digital Computation

To perform division, we use the following:

$$\frac{A}{B} = \frac{F_a}{F_b} 2^{E_a - E_b} \quad (5\text{-}23)$$

That is, when we perform division, we divide the fractional parts and subtract the exponents. For example:

$$\frac{.100001111 \times 2^{11}}{.1011 \times 2^5} = .01101 \times 10^6$$
$$= .1101 \times 10^5$$

5-6. THE ARITHMETIC LOGIC UNIT—ALU

In Sec. 5-1, we discussed a simple ALU that could add two numbers and store their sum. In this section we shall discuss a more complex ALU that can perform many more operations, similar to an ALU in the central processing unit of a small computer.

Where the simple ALU in Fig. 5-3 used D flip-flops in the register, we shall use J-K flip-flops for the more complex ALU since we can easily obtain additional control using them. For each function that we want to obtain, we shall show a simple circuit. After discussing all of the functions, we shall demonstrate how all these simple circuits can be combined. Since all stages of this ALU are identical, we shall work with a single stage. The ALU in Fig. 5-3 consisted of three identical stages.

Our ALU is going to have many control leads. Each of them will be used to control a single function. We shall assume that the signal on all the others is 0. For instance, in Fig. 5-3, there are CLEAR and ADD control leads. If we want the ALU to perform the addition function, then ADD = 1 and CLEAR = 0.

Many signals will be supplied to the J-K flip-flops through a pair of OR gates as shown in Fig. 5-4. The significance of this circuit will be clarified when we discuss the complete ALU.

Addition and Increment by 1

Let's consider a circuit that adds a number, B, to the number stored in the accumulator. We assume that there are $N + 1$ bits stored in the accumulator; the digits of the number B are:

$$b_N b_{N-1} \ldots b_3 b_2 b_1 b_0 \quad (5\text{-}24)$$

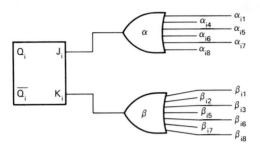

Fig. 5-4. The inputs to the ith flip-flop of the ALU

Now let us consider the stage of the ALU that adds the ith bit and stores the resultant sum. If the digits of the number that is stored in the accumulator are:

$$a_N a_{N-1} \cdots a_3 a_2 a_1 a_0 \qquad (5\text{-}25)$$

then this stage adds $b_i + a_i + c_{i-1}$, where c_{i-1} is the carry from the previous stage. The circuit that we are considering will actually perform two functions. In addition to adding the number B to the contents of the accumulator, it will also add the specific number "one" to the stored contents. (In Sec. 5-3 we saw that adding one was part of taking the 2's complement.) Thus, the circuit will have two control leads: one labled ADD to perform ordinary addition, and one labled INC to increase the contents of the accumulator by one. Consider the operation of this circuit as shown in Fig. 5-5. If the ADD signal is 1, then INC is 0. (Only one control signal will be 1 at any one time.) Then, the b_i input signal will be applied to the b_i input of the full adder FA_i. If the ith bit of B is a 1, then b_i is a 1; if the ith bit is a 0, then b_i is a 0. In addition, one input to each of AND gates a and b will be 1. Hence:

$$J_i = S_i \qquad (5\text{-}26a)$$
$$K_i = \overline{S}_i \qquad (5\text{-}26b)$$

The flip-flop functions as a D flip-flop. Since this circuit functions in essentially the same way as did one stage of the ALU in Fig. 5-3, the desired addition occurs.

Suppose that ADD = 0 and INC = 1. One input to AND gate e will now be 0. Thus, the bit b_i cannot be input. The circuit still functions as an adder with zero input, except for one difference. The c_0 input of the first adder is not used during addition, because there is no carry into the rightmost column. When INC = 1, then the input to c_0 is 1. Note that the first adder takes the sum

Basic Digital Computation

$b_0 + a_0 + c_0$. Thus, a c_0 input acts in the same way as does a b_0. Hence, when INC = 1, then $c_0 = 1$ and one will be added to the number stored in the accumulator. After the next clock pulse, this incremented number will be stored in the accumulator.

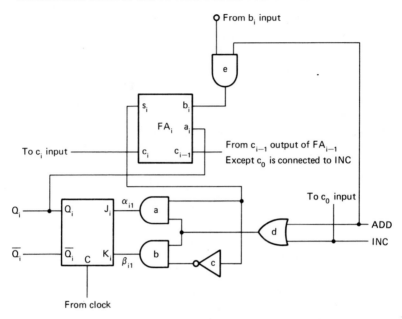

Fig. 5-5. The portion of one stage of the ALU that either performs addition or increments the contents of the register by one

Note the points labled a_{i1} and β_{i1}. Suppose that the flip-flop were replaced by the flip-flop and OR gates in Fig. 5-4. In this case, the output of AND gate a in Fig. 5-5 would be connected to OR gate a input, a_{i1} (Fig. 5-4). Similarly, the output of AND gate b in Fig. 5-5 would be connected to OR gate β input, β_{i1} (Fig. 5-4). Now suppose that all other a_i and β_i are 0's. The circuit would function exactly as did the circuit in Fig. 5-5. Since all the other a_i and β_i are 0, we have:

$$J_i = S_i$$

$$K_i = \overline{S}_i$$

just as before. The inclusion of the OR gates does not change the operation of the circuit since the other a_i and β_i were 0. The presence of the OR gates will allow us to obtain the different ALU functions that we need. Note that when ADD = 0 and INC = 0, then the output is $a_{i1} = \beta_{i1} = 0$. Now, as far as the operation of the OR gates α and β are concerned, the a_{i1} and β_{i1} connection could be removed. The other OR gate inputs can be used to obtain different functions.

Clear

If we want to clear the accumulator, we use the circuit shown in Fig. 5-6. In this case, $J_i = 0$. (Note that there is no J input.) When CLEAR = 1, then $K_i = 1$. Hence, the flip-flop will be set to state $Q_i = 0$ at the next clock pulse. When the flip-flop is replaced by the circuit in Fig. 5-4, CLEAR will be applied to the β_{i2} lead in Fig. 5-4. All the other a_i and β_i inputs will be 0. Hence, when CLEAR = 1, we have $J_i = 0$, $K_i = 1$ and the desired clearing occurs. (Note that we do not need an a_{i2} input since it is zero.)

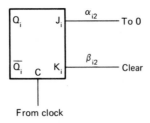

Fig. 5-6. The portion of one stage of the ALU that performs clearing

Logic AND

There are times when we want to perform some logical operations using the b_i input and the number stored in the accumulator. Consider the performance of the logic AND first. The b_i bit of the input binary number B is compared with Q_i, the bit stored in the ith accumulator. If b_i AND Q_i are both 1's, then the value of Q_i remains 1. If either b_i or Q_i or both are 0, then Q_i becomes 0. The circuit that performs this operation is shown in Fig. 5-7. Note that if AND = 1 and $b_i = 1$, then $\beta_{i3} = 0$. Thus, the state of the flip-flop will not change. And, if $Q_i = 1$, then it remains 1 as desired. Similarly, if $Q_i = 0$, then it remains 0. On the other hand, if $b_i = 0$, then when AND = 1, we have $K_i = 1$, $J_i = 0$ and, at the next clock pulse, $Q_i = 0$ as it should. If AND = 0 then $\beta_{i3} = 0$ and there is no change in the state of the flip-flop.

If we replace the flip-flop with the circuit in Fig. 5-4, with β_{i3} connected to the correspondingly marked input of OR gate β, the circuit will function just as we have discussed. Note that if AND = 0, then $\beta_{i3} = 0$ and the input will not interfere with any other inputs.

Basic Digital Computation

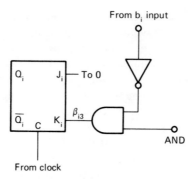

Fig. 5-7. The portion of one stage of the ALU that performs the logic AND operation

Logic OR

The logic OR operation is performed in the following way. The b_i bit of the binary number B is compared with the Q_i bit stored in the accumulator. If either or both of these are 1's, then a 1 will be stored in the ith flip-flop after the next clock pulse. If both Q_i and b_i are 0's, then a 0 will be stored in Q_i. Hence, Q_i will be unchanged unless $b_i = 1$ and $Q_i = 0$. Then, Q_i will be made a 1. A circuit that performs the logic OR operation is shown in Fig. 5-8. When OR = 1, and $Q_i = 1$, then Q_i will remain 1, independent of the value of b_i. If OR = 1 and $Q_i = 0$ with $b_i = 1$, then, at the next clock pulse, Q_i will become 1. Thus, the circuit functions as it should. If OR = 0, then $a_{i4} = 0$; thus, we may replace the flip-flop by the circuit in Fig. 5-4.

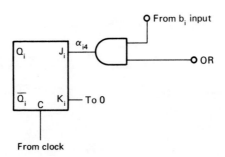

Fig. 5-8. The portion of one stage of the ALU that performs the logic OR operation

Logic XOR

The logic XOR operation is performed in the following way. The b_i bit of the binary number B is compared with the Q_i bit stored in the accumulator. If *either* Q_i *or* b_i is a 1, then, after the next clock pulse, the number stored in the flip-flop will be a 1. If *both* b_i and Q_i are 0's, or if *both* b_i and Q_i are 1's, then, after the next clock pulse, Q_i will be 0. A circuit that implements this operation is shown in Fig. 5-9. If XOR = 1 and b_i = 1, then, after the next clock pulse, the state of the flip-flop changes. Thus, if Q_i was 0, it will become 1; similarly, if it was 1, it will become 0. This is in agreement with the XOR operation. Similarly, if XOR = 1 and b_i = 0 and if Q_i = 0, Q_i will remain 0 and if Q_i = 1, it will remain 1. Thus, the circuit functions as it should for all possible inputs. Finally, if XOR = 0, then α_{i5} and β_{i5} = 0, meaning that we can replace the flip-flop by the circuit in Fig. 5-4.

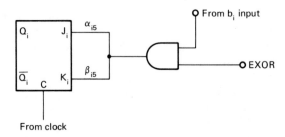

Fig. 5-9. The portion of one stage of the ALU that performs the logic XOR operation

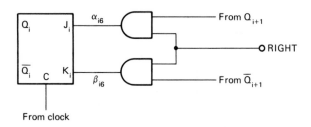

Fig. 5-10. The portion of one stage of the ALU that performs the right shift

Shift Right

Now let's discuss some operations that work with the contents of the accumulator, starting with the shifting operations. These circuits will be similar in operation to the controlled shift register in Fig. 3-30. To shift the contents of the accumulator to the right, the input of each flip-flop must come from the output of the flip-flop immediately to its left. The circuit is shown in Fig. 5-10. Note that the leftmost flip-flop then has no input. For this flip-flop, entered data and its complement replace the Q_{i+1} and $\bar{Q}_{i+1}$ shown in Fig. 5-10. In this case, the accumulator functions as a shift register.

Note that when RIGHT = 1, then the right shift occurs. If RIGHT = 0, then $a_{i6} = \beta_{i6} = 0$ and no shift occurs. Again, we can replace the flip-flop by the circuit in Fig. 5-4.

Shift Left

The circuit which shifts the contents of the accumulator to the left is essentially the same as the right shift circuit except that now the input to a flip-flop comes from the flip-flop immediately to its right. The input to the rightmost flip-flop consists of an external signal and its complement. A circuit that performs the left shift is shown in Fig. 5-11. Again, note that when LEFT = 0, then $a_{i7} = \beta_{i7} = 0$, thus allowing us to replace the flip-flop by the circuit in Fig. 5-4.

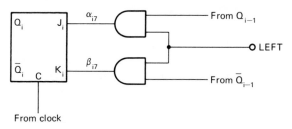

Fig. 5-11. The portion of one stage of the ALU that performs the left shift

Complement

The circuit shown in Fig. 5-12 illustrates how we can complement all the bits stored in the accumulator. This is useful in obtaining the 2's complement. The flip-flop is connected as a T flip-flop. When COMP = 1, it will change its state, complementing its contents. Again, note that when COMP = 0, then $a_{i8} = \beta_{i8} = 0$. We can again replace the flip-flop by the circuit in Fig. 5-4.

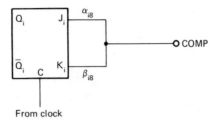

Fig. 5-12. The portion of one stage of the ALU that performs complementation

Interconnection of Inputs

Since we have considered a number of operations here, remember that when the circuits in Figs. 5-5 through 5-12 are connected together, only a *single* control signal can be a 1 at any single time; all the others will be 0. Instead of just using a J-K flip-flop, we use the circuit in Fig. 5-4 where there are separate OR gates connected to the J and K inputs. Then, in each of Figs. 5-5 through 5-12, we break the circuit at the points which are marked α_{ik} and β_{ik} and make the connections to the OR gates as indicated in Fig. 5-4. Each function will operate as before. For instance, suppose that ADD = 1 with all other control signals 0. Then:

$$\alpha_{i4} = \alpha_{i5} = \alpha_{i6} = \alpha_{i7} = \alpha_{i8} = \beta_{i3} = \beta_{i5} = \beta_{i6} = \beta_{i7} = \beta_{i8}$$

Hence:

$$J_i = \alpha_{i1}$$
$$K_i = \beta_{i1}$$

This is exactly the condition in Fig. 5-5 and means that the addition operation will be performed. A similar statement can be made about each of the control signals.

Output Checks

We shall now discuss two other ALU operations which provide us with information about the number stored in the accumulator. They do not change the stored data in any way.

Negative check

We want to have an output signal which is 1 when the number stored in the accumulator is negative and 0 otherwise. We shall assume here that the 2's complement number representation is

Basic Digital Computation

used. Then, the number is negative if its leftmost bit is a 1 and will be positive otherwise. Thus, we only need to examine the state of the leftmost flip-flop to determine if the number is negative.

A circuit that accomplishes this is shown in Fig. 5-13. The control signal is shown here as NEG. When NEG = 1, then γ_1 will equal Q_N. Since Q_N is the leftmost stored bit, γ will equal 1 when the stored number is negative and will equal 0 when the stored number is zero or positive. When NEG = 0, then a negative check is not being performed and $\gamma_1 = 0$.

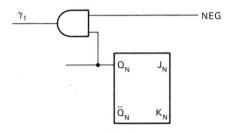

Fig. 5-13. The negative check circuit

Zero check

We also want to be able to check if the stored number is zero. If this is the case, then:

$$Q_0 = Q_1 = Q_2 = \cdots = Q_N = 0 \tag{5-27}$$

In this case:

$$\bar{Q}_0 = \bar{Q}_1 = \bar{Q}_2 = \cdots = \bar{Q}_N = 1 \tag{5-28}$$

The circuit in Fig. 5-14 performs the zero check. When ZERO = 1, then γ_2 will equal 1 only if Eq. (5-28) is satisfied. If $\gamma_2 = 0$ when ZERO = 1, then the number stored in the register is not zero. Note that when ZERO = 0, the output γ_2 will always be 0.

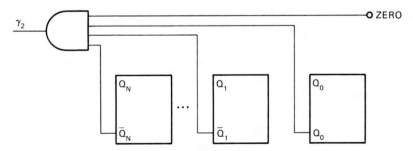

Fig. 5-14. The zero check circuit

We have shown the ALU with an output corresponding to a zero check and an output corresponding to a negative check. Often, ALUs have only one output for both of these circuits. If ZERO = 1, then this output gives the result of the zero check. Similarly, if NEG = 1, this output gives the result of the negative check. Such a single output can be obtained by connecting γ_1 and γ_2 in Figs. 5-13 and 5-14 to separate inputs of a two-input OR gate (Fig. 5-15). Remember that a zero check and a negative check will not be made at the same time.

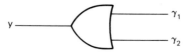

Fig. 5-15. A circuit that provides a single output for the zero check and negative check signals

In this section we have discussed a simple complete ALU that performs many functions. We have not discussed every possible function that can be performed by an ALU. However, we have discussed the common ones. More important, an understanding of these operations should enable you to understand other ALUs, even if they perform additional operations. In the next chapter we shall see how the ALU fits into a complete computer.

EXERCISES

5-1. Describe the function of a simple ALU.

5-2. Describe the operation of the adder in Fig. 5-2 in your own words.

5-3. Draw a circuit for a four-bit adder.

5-4. Completely describe the operation of the three-bit ALU in Fig. 5-3.

5-5. Modify the ALU in Fig. 5-3 so that it can store and add four-bit numbers.

5-6. Numbers are stored in a four-bit binary register. Obtain three numbers which are equivalent on a modulo 16 basis to the stored number 0110_2.

5-7. Write four numbers that are equivalent, modulo 128, to 4_{10}, 16_{10}, 1100_2, and 11111_2.

5-8. Using the procedures discussed in Sec. 5-3, perform the subtraction $1101 - 1011$.

Basic Digital Computation

5-9. Repeat Exercise 5-8, subtracting $110011 - 011111$.

5-10. Discuss how the modular properties of registers can be used to advantage.

5-11. Obtain the 2's complement of the following binary numbers:

$$110011, \quad 1011, \quad 1100111$$

5-12. Use the 2's complement to obtain a binary representation of the whole numbers from -15 to $+15$. Use four bits.

5-13. Repeat Exercise 5-8, using the 2's complement.

5-14. Repeat Exercise 5-9, using the 2's complement.

5-15. Perform the following multiplication:

$$(011101)(011010)$$

5-16. Verify the multiplication of Exercise 5-15 by dividing the answer by 011010.

5-17. Discuss the nature and cause of a true overflow. Why should it be avoided?

5-18. What is the base 10 equivalent of

$$0.1101 \times 2^6$$

5-19. Repeat Exercise 5-18 for

$$.01101 \times 2^{-6}$$

5-20 Discuss the meaning of significant figures.

5-21. Add the following two numbers:

$$A = .11011 \times 2^6$$
$$B = .11101 \times 2^7$$

5-22. Multiply the two numbers given in Exercise 5-21.

5-23. Verify the multiplication in Exercise 5-22 by dividing the answer obtained there by $.11011 \times 2^6$.

5-24. Discuss the reasons for roundoff error in digital computations.

5-25. Discuss the operation of the circuit in Fig. 5-5.

5-26. Discuss the operation of the circuit in Fig. 5-6.

5-27. Discuss the operation of the circuit in Fig. 5-7.

5-28. Discuss the operation of the circuit in Fig. 5-8.

5-29. Discuss the operation of the circuit in Fig. 5-9.

5-30. Discuss the operation of the circuit in Fig. 5-10.

5-31. Discuss the operation of the circuit in Fig. 5-11.

5-32. Discuss the operation of the circuit in Fig. 5-12.

5-33. Discuss how the functions of the circuits in Figs. 5-5 through 5-12 can be combined in a single ALU.

5-34. Discuss the operation of the negative check circuit.

5-35. Discuss the operation of the zero check circuit.

5-36. Discuss how the output of the negative check and zero check circuits can be combined into a single output.

6 The Digital Computer

It is the object of this chapter to provide a thorough understanding of the operation of the digital computer from both a "hardware" and a "software" point of view. Beginning with the general organization of the computer, we shall discuss the way in which instructions are stored, the nature and development of a machine language, and the practical task of writing a machine language program. We shall also describe loaders, assembler languages, and higher level languages.

6-1. THE GENERAL ORGANIZATION OF A DIGITAL COMPUTER

The block diagram in Fig. 6-1 can be used to describe the general organization of a digital computer. There are four basic units. All computations are performed in the arithmetic logic unit, ALU. In a small computer, this unit would consist of an ALU of the type discussed in Sec. 5-6, possibly with an additional register(s); the ALU in many computers (even small ones) often contain several accumulators. We have already discussed all the types of circuits that would be used in an ALU.

In Sec. 5-6 we saw that the ALU performed functions selected by a set of control signals such as ADD, CLEAR, and OR. These signals are generated by a *control unit*, which receives its instructions from the program. We shall subsequently discuss how this information is supplied to the computer. Some control units are more complex than others. For instance, in Sec. 5-3 we discussed performing subtraction by complementing the subtrahend, adding 1 to it, and then adding the resulting number to the minuend.

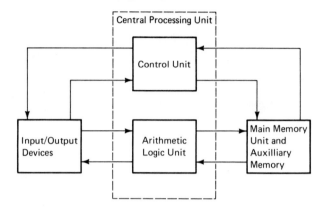

Fig. 6-1. A block diagram of the basic computer

Three separate instructions had to be supplied to the ALU: Complement, Increment by 1, and Add. If the control unit were a simple one, then these three instructions would have to be provided by the program. With more complex control units, only a single command to subtract need be supplied. The control unit would then generate the three control signals in the proper sequence and at the proper times.

In addition to controlling the supply of data from or to the input/output devices, the control unit also directs the reading/writing functions of the memory. The control unit also contains the master clock which synchronizes the operation of all parts of the computer. Note the dashed line in Fig. 6-1 that goes around both the control unit and the ALU.; in very small computers, these are both found in a single LSI semiconductor chip. In such cases, this is called a *microprocessor*. In any event, the ALU and the control unit comprise the *central processing unit*, CPU.

The memory can be broken into two parts. The main memory unit, MMU, is a random access memory like the ones discussed in Chapter 4. In most small computers it consists of a semiconductor memory although core memories are occasionally used. There are also auxiliary tape and disk memories, which we discussed in Chapter 4.

In order to use the computer, we must be able to supply it with programs and data. After computation is complete, it must be able to supply us with the results. Communication with the computer is the function of the input/output devices. The simplest input devices consist of a set of toggle switches on the computer. When they are up, they correspond to 1's, and when they are down, they correspond to 0's. Thus, these toggle switches can be set to represent a binary number. Such binary numbers can represent either a single instruction of a particular program or simply data to be processed. We shall subsequently discuss how this information can be stored in any memory location. Using toggle switches to input data is called *toggling*.

It is much easier to use other forms of input. For example, a terminal allows the programmer to type in his program; the terminal generates a sequence of 0's and 1's which the computer interprets. Other forms of input devices use magnetic tapes and disks where the sequences of 0's and 1's are stored on a magnetic film as discussed in Sec. 4-5. Note that magnetic tape and disk storage can be considered as both an input/output device and as an auxiliary memory. If they are are to supply data or programs, or if the final results of the computations are stored by them, then they are input/output devices; if they store such things as intermediate results, they can be considered to be part of the memory. Large computers often use card readers as their input devices; here the data is stored in holes on punched cards.

There are special purpose input devices. For instance, there are scanners at supermarket checkouts that can read the lines that are now marked on grocery items. These scanners supply data to the computer which then computes the total bill while also performing such functions as keeping track of inventory.

The output device could be the same terminal that was used for data input. A disadvantage of some terminals is that they are slow and noisy. The line printer is a much faster output device which prints an entire line at a time, whereas the terminal only prints one character at a time. The video terminal, another device, is also much faster and quieter than the mechanical terminal. Here the information is presented on a television-like screen; the device usually has a keyboard so that it can be used for both input and output. The major disadvantage of the simple video terminal is that it does not provide a printed copy (hard copy).

In many cases, both the input and the output of data is different from what we have discussed. For instance, the input data could come from temperature, sunlight level, and humidity sensors which are located at many points inside and outside a large building. Or the output could consist of signals that control relays which activate heaters and humidifiers in the building.

Buses

Although we have shown only two lines connecting the various parts of the computer in Fig. 6-1, there are actually many wires that run between the various parts. This collection of wires is called a *bus*. Suppose that the computer uses 16 bit words. In the bus, there must then be a wire for each bit. In Sec. 4-1 we learned that there must be one input line for each binary address used by the memory. For instance, in Fig. 4-3, we have two input address lines for a four-word memory. In additon, there must be a chip select line, and finally read/write lines for the memory. All of these constitute additional lines for the bus.

In Sec. 5-6, we discussed the use of a separate control line for each function of the ALU. Each of these control lines must also be included in the bus as well as any other control lines, such as bus leads for clock signals. Since the computer circuits are run on direct current, the bus contains these power supply leads. And, finally, to allow for computer expansion, such as an increase in memory capacity, a bus will also contain extra leads. Some small computers have as many as 100 lead buses.

It may appear as though all the leads of the bus need not be run to all the parts of the computer. However, the bus is often built as a wide plastic strip with foil wires embedded in it. It is convenient to use this same bus throughout the computer since it provides a very versatile arrangement. In small computers, the bus often consists of a set of "wires" printed on a circuit board called the *mother board*. This provides access to all the leads of the computer, since connectors can be attached to the board. Again, this is done for versatility. For instance, new components can be added by plugging them into the bus.

6-2. MEMORY COMMANDS—INFORMATION TRANSMISSION

In Sec. 5-6, we discussed the various functions that the ALU can perform. In Sec. 6-5 we shall see how these commands are incorporated into a machine language program which is stored in the computer and directs its operation. In this section we shall discuss the details of how commands are stored in the computer, in particular some specific commands that are used to control the memory.

Let's begin by considering how the memory is addressed. In Sec. 4-1, we saw that the address of the word to be read or written is supplied in binary. There is a lead for each binary digit of the

The Digital Computer

address. To address the memory, the appropriate signals are placed on the address line of the bus. There is a register called the *memory address register* (MAR) that stores, in binary, the address of the memory location that is to be used. That is, the address leads of the bus supply the input for the MAR. The MAR will contain the address of either the word to be read or the word to be written. In Fig. 4-3 we show a memory (flip-flop) that can be used for a MAR.

There is another register called the *memory buffer register* (MBR) that is also associated with the main memory. If writing into the memory is to be performed, then the MBR stores the word that is to be written. If the memory is read, then the word that has just been read is stored in the MBR.

Only a few commands are required to operate the memory:

1. Write the word stored in the MBR into the main memory in the location specified in the MAR. (6-1)

2. Read the word stored in the location in the MAR into the MBR. (6-2)

3. Clear or enter a word into the MAR (6-3)

At times, in simple computers, these commands are combined with others. For instance, we shall discuss a command to store the contents of the ALU in the memory location specified in the command. Actually, this single instruction might take the place of several commands, one to store the contents of the MBR in the MBR, and then one to store the contents of the MBR in the specified memory location. However, this sequence of commands would automatically be generated by the control unit. Actually, some simple computers may not have MBRs and they may utilize other registers, such as the one in the ALU.

Word Structure

In considering the structure of the words stored in the memory, remember that there are two types of information which are stored: instructions and data. The data is either a stored number, which may be a floating point number, or a number without an exponent; or it is a code for alphanumeric information.

Each stored instruction word usually contains an instruction and a memory location; some computers, however, will use more complex words which may contain further information. Each instruction has a binary code. For instance, 000001 could indicate that the contents of the specified memory location should be added to the contents of the accumulator.

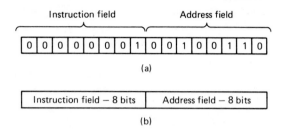

Fig. 6-2. (a) A sixteen bit word with an 8 bit instruction field and an 8 bit address field; (b) A short hand representation of this word

To illustrate this, we shall work with a 16 bit word, as shown in Fig. 6-2a. (Figure 6-2b is a simpler representation of the word structure.) The word is broken into two subwords called *fields*. One field is used to express the instruction, and the other field contains the memory location. Consider the specific word in Fig. 6-2:

$$00000001\ \ 00100110_2 \qquad (6\text{-}4)$$

The first 8 bits represent the instruction and the last 8 bits represent the memory location. The first 8 bits 00000001 instruct the computer to add the contents of the specified memory location to the contents of the ALU. The last 8 bits:

$$00100110_2$$

specify a memory location. Word (6-4) means to add the contents of memory location 00100110_2 (38_{10}) to the number previously stored in the accumulator. The instruction field contains a binary number that represents an instruction. This is called an *operational code* or *op-code*.

The word (6-4) represents one statement of a *machine language program*, a program written in binary which directs the operation of the computer. To eliminate any possible confusion or error due to the number of digits, it is customary to write the program in octal or hexadecimal. For instance:

$$00100110_2 = 045_8 = 20_{16} \qquad (6\text{-}5)$$

The octal or hexadecimal representation is much easier to handle, and many machine language programs are written in octal or hexadecimal. The actual program, of course, is in binary.

We have discussed a word which has an instruction field and an address field. This word structure is used to direct the computer to perform an operation (possibly) in conjunction with a memory location. In the previous example, the instruction caused the contents of the specified memory location to be added to the contents of the accumulator. Another instruction could be to store the contents of the accumulator in a specified memory location.

We shall use this word structure in subsequent examples because it is simple. This will eliminate unnecessary detail from our discussion. However, other types of structure can be used. For instance, some computers use words with two addresses. Suppose that we wanted to transfer the contents of one memory location to another memory location, a word with two address fields could be used to do this with a single instruction.

There are other procedures for instructing computers. Many small computers use 8 bit words. If 8 or more bits are used to specify the memory location, an 8 bit word cannot provide for both an instruction field (op-code) and an address field. These small computers use a sequence of words to make up the entire instruction. For example, suppose that there are two words in the sequence. The first word would supply the op-code and the second word would supply the address of the specified memory location. An 8 bit word can be used to specify 256 addresses. Actually, most small computers have many more addresses than this; often 16 bits are used to specify the addresses (65,536 locations can then be addressed). In such cases, each instruction consists of a sequence of three words. The first supplies the op-code while the next two give the memory location. In this example, the instruction consisted of 24 bits and is said to consist of three 8 bit bytes.

When you program your computer, the structure of the instruction must be known. The instruction manual that comes with the computer will provide these details.

6-3. ENTERING AND EXECUTION OF INSTRUCTIONS

In learning how a program is entered and how the instructions are executed, we shall work with a very simple procedure in this section. In a subsequent section, however, we shall discuss more sophisticated methods which will greatly facilitate programming for the user. However, the other ideas that we shall discuss here are applicable to all computers.

The most elementary form of program or data input is called *toggling*. As discussed in Sec. 6-1, some computers have switches on their front panels. One switch is provided for each bit of the word. When the switches are up, they represent 1's; when they are down, they represent 0's. To enter a word, we need only throw all the toggle switches into the correct positions. To make it convenient for the programmer, these switches are usually arranged in groups of three or four. This makes it easy to write the program in octal or hexadecimal while still entering the data in binary. When we enter a program, instructions and data are stored in separate memory locations. With the elementary system for entering information that we are using in this section, we must specify the memory location. Usually, the following procedure is used. The toggle switches are set to specify a memory location (in binary) and a button is pressed. Next, the desired instruction or data that is to be stored in the memory is set up on the toggle switches. A button is pressed and this number is then stored in the previously specified memory location. Because this procedure must be repeated for *each* instruction or word of data, it is rather tedious. Much simpler ways to enter information will be described later.

Execution of Instructions

To illustrate the execution of instructions, we shall write out a simple machine language program, specifying some additional instructions. For instructional purposes a 16 bit word will be used. The commands are:

add contents of specified memory location to accumulator	$0000\ 0001_2 = 01_{16}$	(6-6a)
clear accumulator	$0000\ 0010_2 = 02_{16}$	(6-6b)
put contents of accumulator in specified memory location	$0001\ 0100_2 = 14_{16}$	(6-6c)
stop computation	$0111\ 0111_2 = 77_{16}$	(6-6d)

Now let us write a very simple program. We shall assume that the computer executes instructions in order, that is, it executes the instruction in memory location 1 first, next it executes the instruction in memory location 2, and so on. In this simple program we shall list both the instructions and the memory locations in which they are stored. They have been toggled in as we discussed earlier. Both binary and hexadecimal notation are used.

Table 6-1: An Elementary Program

Memory location		Stored word	
Binary	Hexadecimal	Binary	Hexadecimal
00000001	01	0000001000000000	0200
00000010	02	0000000100010000	0110
00000011	03	0000000100010001	0111
00000100	04	0001010000010010	1412
00000101	05	0111011100000000	7700
00010000	10	0000000000000011	0003
00010001	11	0000000000000100	0004

In the operation of this program, remember that the first 8 bits of the instruction specify the actual instruction. The next 8 bits specify a memory location. Our first instruction is

$$0200_{16}$$

The 02_{16} is the command to clear the accumulator. The memory location has no significance here and the last two hexadecimal digits are actually ignored by the computer. We could use any number there.

The next command is

$$0110_{16}$$

The 01_{16} command indicates that the number stored in memory location $10_{16} = 16_{10}$ is to be added to the accumulator. The number stored in memory location 10_{16} is

$$0000000000000011_2 = 0003_{16} = 3_{10}$$

Hence, after the command is executed, 00003_{16} will be in the accumulator. (It is stored, of course, in binary.)

The next command is

$$0111_{16}$$

which specifies that the contents of memory location 11_{16} is added to the accumulator. The number stored in memory location 11_{16} is

$$0000000000000100_2 = 00004_{16} = 4_{10}$$

After the command is executed the number stored in the accumulator will be previously stored number plus 0000000000000100_2. In hexadecimal notation this will be:

$$3_{16} + 4_{16} = 7_{16} = 7_{10}$$

The next command is

$$1412_{16}$$

The 14_{16} indicates that the contents of the accumulator is to be stored in the memory location 12_{16}. After the command is executed, the word stored in memory location $12_{16} = 18_{10}$ would be

$$0000000000000111_2 = 7_{16} = 7_{10}$$

The next command executed is

$$7700_{16}$$

The 77 causes compuation to cease, and the result of the computation is now stored in memory location 12_{16}. In this simple program, we did not consider the output of data. We shall do so in Sec. 6-5.

Let us consider some of the operations of the computer in greater detail. The op-code instructs the computer to perform a specific operation. When the instruction is executed, the appropriate control signal is supplied to the ALU. (The ALU and its control signals were discussed in Sec. 5-6.) Let us see how this is accomplished using our simple computer as an example. The 8 leftmost bits of the instruction (i.e., the op-code) are stored in a register called the *instruction register* (IR). (The remaining 8 bits are stored in the memory address register (MAR).) An *instruction decoder* converts the information stored in the IR to the appropriate control signal. A simple one is diagrammed in Fig. 6-3. It decodes the op-code

$$b_7 b_6 b_5 b_4 b_3 b_2 b_1 b_0 \qquad (6\text{-}7)$$

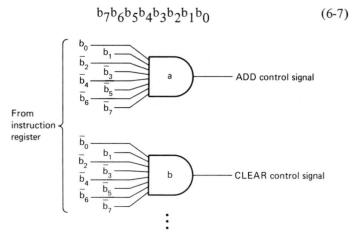

Fig. 6-3. A portion of the control signal decoder

For instance, if the op-code is 00000001, then the output of AND gate a will be a 1, and the ADD control signal will be a 1. All the other control signals will be 0. Similarly, if the number stored in the instruction register is 00000010, then the output of AND gate b will be a 1 and the CLEAR control signal will be given.

When a program is executed, the number stored in each memory location is merely a sequence of 0's and 1's. This number carries no information to indicate if it is an instruction or if it is data. It is only the order in which the word is read that indicates this. For instance, suppose that 0110_{16} is read from the memory location and that this is to be treated as a command. This indicates that the contents of memory location 10_{16} is to be added to the accumulator. When the contents of memory location 10_{16} are read from the memory location, this is to be treated as data. Thus, the contents of one memory location is a command while the contents of the other is data. Let's see how the computer keeps track of this.

There is a one-bit register in the control unit called a *fetch-execute register* (FER). Its function is to indicate to the computer whether it is "fetching" an instruction from the memory or executing an instruction (information extracted from the memory is data). If the contents of the FER is a 1, then the computer treats the information being extracted from memory as an instruction. If the contents of the FER is a 0, then the information is treated as data. Before describing the operation of the FER, let us describe another register, called the *program counter* (PC), which holds the address of the instruction being executed. Whenever an instruction is executed, the program goes through a series of steps. In addition to the steps used to carry out the instruction, there are additional operations which increase the number stored in the PC by one.

Now let us consider the execution of a program. When the operation is started, the contents of the FER is set to 1. In addition, the contents of the PC is set to 00000001. (We are working with our 8 bit address computer here.) Since the contents of the FER is a 1, the information fetched from the memory is treated as an instruction. Since the contents of PC = 00000001, the contents of memory location 01_{16} is fetched. The leftmost 8 bits are put into the IR and the rightmost 8 bits are put into the memory address register (MAR). Now the computer is put into its execute phase. The contents of the FER is set to 0. The contents of the IR is input to the instruction decoder and the appropriate control signal is generated. The address stored in the MAR is read and the instruction designated by the op-code (stored in the IR) is carried out. Hence, the desired instruction is performed. Now the contents of the FER is set to 1 again and the contents of the PC is incremented by 1 so that it becomes $00000010_2 = 02_{16}$. Now the information stored in memory location 02_{16} is fetched and treated as an instruction. This process is then repeated. The sequence of operations that we have described here may vary. For instance, the PC contents may be incremented much earlier in the sequence of steps.

Note that we have described a simple program counter operation where it increases by 1 after each instruction. Usually, computers have instructions that can be used to change the value stored in the PC, meaning that program need not be executed in sequence. This greatly increases the versatility of the computer.

Remember that the computer cannot tell the difference between instructions and data. For example, suppose that the third statement of the program in Table 6-1 were changed to

$$0101_{16}$$

Now the contents of memory location 01_{16}, which was the instruction to clear the accumulator, would be added to the accumulator. The value stored in memory location 01_{16} is 0200_{16}. Thus, after the third instruction was executed, the contents of the accumulator would be:

$$0200_{16} + 0003_{16} = 0203_{16}$$

After execution is complete this value would be stored in memory address 12_{16}.

In this example, we read an instruction and used it as data. There can be serious consequences to an operation like this. Suppose that, instead of reading an instruction, we accidentally wrote data into the location of an instruction that had not, as yet, been executed. When that command is subsequently executed, in all probability, there will not be a valid instruction code there. In such cases, the instruction decoder will not output a control signal, the absence of which usually causes computation to cease with an indication of error. Even if, by chance, there is a valid instruction code stored, it will not be the one you want and an error will result.

6-4. THE COMPLETE DIGITAL COMPUTER

We are now ready to talk about a complete digital computer. We shall use the 16-bit word digital computer that we have dis-

The Digital Computer

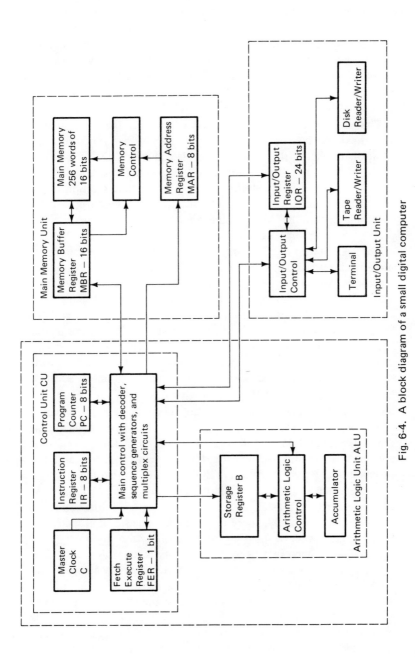

Fig. 6-4. A block diagram of a small digital computer

cussed, noting that the theories of operation can be applied to any wordsize computer. The block diagram for our very small computer is shown in Fig. 6-4. Although we show single lines interconnecting the various parts of the computer, remember that they represent buses composed of many wires. Now let us discuss the various components of the computer. We shall only briefly mention those that have been discussed in detail previously.

The arithmetic logic unit (ALU) consists of the accumulator and the logic circuits used to obtain the desired functions. An additional register, the B register, is also shown. This can be used to store the number that is added to the accumulator. Usually, the ALU is arranged with additional registers so that multiplication and division can be easily carried out. Note that the output of the accumulator can be routed through the control unit to various parts of the computer such as the memory.

The *memory unit* (MU) contains the main memory. Since we assume 8 address lines, we have used a 256-word memory. Computer memories with many more words would require more address leads. However, 256 words serve as an illustration here. The memory control is the type discussed in Chapter 4. An address from the control unit is placed in the MAR; if a "read" command is given, it causes the word stored in that address to be stored in the MBR; or if a "write" command is given, it causes the word stored in the MBR to be stored in the specified memory address.

The *control unit* (CU) directs the operation of the entire computer. It contains the instruction decoder (Fig. 6-3) which "translates" the supplied instruction into control signals that direct the operation of the ALU. Also found in the control unit are the instruction register, the fetch-execute register, and the program counter, all discussed in detail in the last section.

The *master clock* is also part of the control unit. We have explained how the master clock keeps the parts of the computer synchronized. Actually, there is more than one set of clock pulses because certain parts of the computer function at much faster speeds than others. In general, the memory is the slowest. Usually, a single word is read from the memory, followed by the performance of several operations that do not involve the memory. It would be a waste of time if all of these operations were slowed down to the speed of the memory cycle, and for this reason, the master clock often generates several sets of pulses. For example, in Fig. 6-5, we show two, one much faster than the other. However, their relationship to each other is kept constant. Thus, C_1 would be used to clock the high speed parts of the computer and C_2, the memory. This assumes, of course, that there are several operations of the faster parts of the computer for each cycle of the memory. The control unit must contain circuits to insure that the memory is not called upon before it is ready to function.

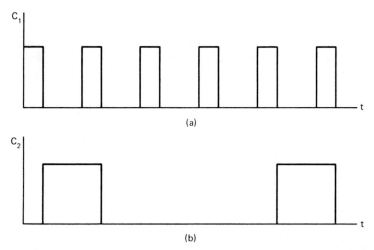

Fig. 6-5. Clock pulses; (a) Normal timing; (b) Slower timing used to control the memory

The input/output unit contains all of the input/output devices. We have only shown a terminal, tape reader/writer, and a disk reader/writer in the block diagram. Actually, there could be other devices such as a video terminal, graph plotter, card reader, and line printer. In addition, there may be other input/output devices. For instance, as discussed in Sec. 6-1, signals from temperature sensors could provide input to the computer. The computer would then provide output to circuits that control heaters, air conditioners, and blowers.

Although we have shown only a small register associated with the input/output unit, there may actually be a relatively large amount of storage there. The input/output devices are usually much slower than all other parts of the computer. For instance, the computer may output data at a much faster rate than can be printed by the terminal. The data, in this case, would be stored in the memory of an input/output device called a *buffer*. The terminal would then take data from the buffer at its own rate. (The buffer can actually be part of the RAM.) If there were no buffer, then each time data was output, the computer would have to pause until the terminal printed out the data. The use of the input/output buffer eliminates the need for many of these pauses.

When data is input to the buffer, it occupies storage space. When the data is read from the buffer and printed by the terminal, this storage space is emptied and the buffer can receive new data. If the buffer is full, then it cannot receive new data and the computer must pause. (Alternatively, data can, at times, be stored in the main memory for later output to the buffer.) We shall discuss this further in the next section when we discuss programming for input/output devices.

6-5. MACHINE LANGUAGE PROGRAMMING

In this section we shall present a short machine language and see how it is used. Machine languages are not standard and the one presented is not a language for any particular computer. The ideas described here, however, are applicable to all computers. We shall base much of our machine language on the commands that can be given to the ALU discussed in Sec. 5-6. In addition, we shall add some other useful commands that are used in almost all computers. At the start we shall not specify any input/output commands. These will be discussed later in this section.

Table 6-2: A Simple Machine Language

Instruction	Code	
	Binary	Hexadecimal
Add contents of specified memory location to accumulator	00000001	01
Clear accumulator	00000010	02
Logical AND	00000011	03
Logical OR	00000100	04
Logical XOR	00000101	05
Shift right	00000110	06
Shift left	00000111	07
Complement	00010000	10
Increment	00010001	11
Negative check	00010010	12
Zero check	00010011	13
Put in specified memory location	00010100	14

Branch unconditionally	00100000	20
Branch on zero	00100001	21
Branch on negative	00100010	22
Continue	00000000	00
Stop computation	01111111	77

Remember that, in our simple computer, the instruction word contained 16 bits. The first (leftmost) 8 of these are the instructions in Table 6-2. The remaining 8 bits contain a memory location. For some instructions, the memory location is not appropriate and should be given as 00000000. Actually, any number could be given here since the computer will ignore it.

The first eleven instructions were discussed in Sec. 5-6 in terms of ALU commands and further described in Secs. 6-2 and 6-3. In addition, the instruction to store the accumulator contents in specified memory location, 14, and the one to stop computation, 77, were also discussed in Sec. 6-3. After briefly explaining the new instructions, we shall illustrate machine language programming by writing some sample programs.

The next to last command is 00, continue. This is an instruction to do nothing; the computer goes on to the next instruction. It is sometimes convenient to use such an instruction. The other new commands all involve branching. The *branch unconditionally* command causes the contents of the program counter to be changed. Remember that the PC contains the contents of the memory location from which the *next* instruction is to be fetched. Normally, PC increases by 1 with each instruction. However, there are times when we want to "jump about" in a program. The unconditional branch instruction allows us to do this. For instance, consider the instruction

$$0010000001000000_2 = 2040_{16}$$

The PC would be set to 40_{16}. If there are no other branching commands, then, after the execution of the instruction which was in memory location 40_{16}, the PC would be incremented by 1 as usual. Hence, the instruction in memory location 41_{16} would be executed next.

The other two branch commands are called *conditional branching*. They function in a manner similar to unconditional branching except that the occurrence of branching depends upon the value stored in the accumulator. For example, suppose that PC = 04_{16} and that the instruction being executed is

$$2142_{16}$$

This is a branch on zero. If the value stored in the accumulator is 0, then PC will be set to 42_{16}. The next instruction will be taken from this address. On the other hand, if the number stored in the accumulator were *not* zero, then the branch on zero command would be *ignored*. That is, the PC would be set to 05_{16} and that would be the location of the next instruction.

The branch on negative instruction works in essentially the same way as the branch on zero command except that now the branching occurs if the contents of the accumulator is negative.

Simple Programs

To illustrate the ideas that we have discussed, we shall write two simple machine language programs. Our object here is not to teach programming, but to explain machine language and computer operation.

In the first program, we begin by subtracting a number N_1 from another number N_2. If the result is negative, then 10_{10} is added to the number, while if the result of the subtraction is positive, or zero, 5_{10} is added to the number. After doing all of this, the result is added to another number N_3. The program and the memory locations of the stored words are given in Table 6-3.

Table 6-3: A Simple Program

Memory Location Hexadecimal	Stored word Binary	Stored word Hexadecimal	Comment
1	0000001000000000	0200	Clear accumulator
2	0000000110010001	0191	Enter subtrahend
3	0001000000000000	1000	Complement subtrahend
4	0001000100000000	1100	Add 1 (2's complement of subtrahend completed)
5	0000000110010010	0192	Add minuend
6	0010001001010000	2250	Branch on negative
7	0000000101010111	0157	Add contents of memory location 57_{16} to accumulator

8	0000000000000000	0000	Continue
9	0000000110010011	0193	Add contents of memory location 93_{16} to accumulator
A	0111011100000000	7700	Stop
50	0000000101100010	0162	Add contents of memory location 62_{16} to accumulator
51	0010000000001000	2008	Branch unconditional to memory location 08_{16} (set PC to 08_{16})
57	0000000000000101	0005	$5_{16} = 5_{10}$
62	0000000000001010	000A	$A_{16} = 10_{10}$
91	0000000000000001	0001	$1_{16} = 1_{10}$
92	0000000000000111	0007	$7_{16} = 7_{10}$
93	0000000000001001	0009	$9_{16} = 9_{10}$

Let us consider the operation of this program. The numbers N_1, N_2, and N_3 are stored in memory locations 91_{16}, 92_{16}, and 93_{16}, respectively. These numbers are:

$$N_1 = 1_{16} = 1_{10}$$
$$N_2 = 7_{16} = 7_{10}$$
$$N_3 = 9_{16} = 9_{10}$$

Now we shall go through the program on a step by step basis. The command in memory location 1_{16} causes the accumulator to be cleared. The value stored there is zero. The second command (memory location 2_{16}) causes the contents of memory location 91_{16} to be added to the accumulator. This is N_1, which we must subtract from N_2. To do this, its 2's complement is obtained by complementing it and adding one to the result. The next two instructions in memory locations 3_{16} and 4_{16} accomplish this. The accumulator now stores $-N_1$.

The next command (memory location 5_{16}) causes the contents of memory location 92_{16} to be added to the accumulator. This adds N_2. Thus, we have now taken $N_2 - N_1$; now we branch on negative (memory location 6_{16}). That is, if the number stored in the accumulator is negative, then the program branches to memory location 50_{16}. If the number stored in the accumulator is not negative, then the next instruction executed is that in memory location number 7_{16}. This causes the contents of memory location 57_{16} to be added to the accumulator. We have stored 5_{10} there so 5 is added to the accumulator. Hence, we now have $N_2 - N_1 + 5$.

The instruction in memory location 8_{16} is "continue". The computer then goes on to the next instruction. We shall see that we branch back to this instruction.

The next instruction executed is that in memory location number 9_{16}. This causes the contents of memory location 93_{16} to be added to the accumulator. We have, at this point, performed the operation $N_2 - N_1 + 5 + N_3$. Computation is now complete and the computer is stopped. Actually, in a practical program, we would not stop at this point since there would be an instruction to output the data. But we have not included such a command here because we have not yet discussed the output of data.

Now go back to the branching instruction in memory location 6_{16}. Suppose that we had different values stored in memory locations 91_{16} and 92_{16} so that $N_2 - N_1$ was negative. Then, the next statement executed would be the one stored in memory location 50_{16}. This instruction is to add the contents of memory location number 62_{16} to the accumulator. The contents of memory location 62_{16} is 10_{10}. Thus, if $N_2 - N_1$ is negative, we perform $N_2 - N_1 + 10$.

After this is done, the instruction just executed was in memory location 50_{16}. Therefore, the next instruction to be executed lies in memory location 51_{16}. This is an unconditional branch which sets the program counter to 8_{16}. The next instruction executed lies in this memory location. It is the "continue" statement. After this, the next instruction executed is that in memory location 9_{16}. As discussed, this adds N_3 and the computation stops. Thus, we have taken $N_2 - N_1 + 10 + N_3$.

Suppose that we want to change the data and run the program again. Since the data is stored in memory locations 91_{16}, 92_{16}, and 93_{16}, we eould only have to change the values stored in these three locations without having to change the rest of the program. This is a great convenience, especially if the program is long.

Consider another example of machine language programming. Suppose that we want to take the sum

$$1 + 2 + 3 + 4 + \cdots + 98 + 99 + 100$$

A program that does this directly would have many steps and be very tedious for the programmer. The following program uses branching to shorten the program and eliminate the tedium.

Table 6-4: Program for the Computation of $1 + 2 + 3 + \cdots + 98 + 99 + 100$

Memory location Hexadecimal	Stored word Hexadecimal	Binary
1	0200	0000001000000000
2	0181	0000000110000001
3	1100	0001000100000000
4	1481	0001010010000001
5	1000	1000000000000000
6	1100	1000100000000000
7	0180	0000000110000000
8	2190	0010000110010000
9	0200	0000001000000000
A	0181	0000000110000001
B	0182	0000000110000010
C	1482	0001010010000010
D	2001	0010000000000001
80	0065	0000000001100101
81	0000	0000000000000000
82	0000	0000000000000000
90	7700	0111011100000000

Operation of this program begins with clearing the accumulator (instruction in memory location 1_{16}). The next instruction (in memory location 2_{16}) causes the contents of memory location 81_{16} to be added to the accumulator. At the start, this number is zero. The contents of this memory location will be the next number to be added to the sum. The next command (in memory location 3_{16}) adds one to the contents of the accumulator. The next instruction (in memory location 4_{16}) causes this number to be stored in memory location 81_{16} (the old value is erased).

The number just stored in memory location 81_{16} will eventually be added to the sum, but we must check to see if it is greater than 100_{10}. To do this, the contents of the accumulator are complemented (instruction in memory location 5_{16}) and then incremented (instruction in memory location 6_{16}). We have thus taken the 2's complement of the number we want to check. The instruction in memory location 7_{16} causes the number stored in memory location 80_{16} to be added to the 2's complement. Note that this stored number is 101_{10}. If the contents of the accumulator after the "subtraction" is zero, we must not add the number stored in memory location 81_{16} to the sum. The instruction in memory location 8_{16} is a branch on zero. If the number stored in memory location 81_{16} were 101_{10}, then, after 2's complementing it and adding it to 101_{10}, the result would be zero. In this case, because of the branch on zero command, the next instruction executed would be stored in memory location 90_{16}. The instruction stored there, 77_{16}, signifies "stop." Thus, if the number stored in memory location 81_{16} were 101_{10}, we stop and the computation is complete. But if the last number stored there were less than 101_{10}, then computation would continue.

Now let us return to the instruction in memory location 8_{16} and assume that the branch on zero failed. Then, the next instruction executed would be the one in memory location 9_{16}. This is 02_{16}, which causes the accumulator to be cleared.

Next, according to the instruction in memory location A_{16}, the contents of memory location 81_{16} are added to the accumulator. Note that, after the first step, this is now 1. Next (instruction in memory location B_{16}), the contents of memory location 82_{16} are added to the accumulator. This is still zero.

The next instruction (memory location C_{16}) causes the contents of the accumulator to be put into memory location number 82_{16}. This number, still in the accumulator, is 1_{10}. This is the first sum.

The next command (memory location D_{16}) causes the program to branch unconditionally back to memory location 1_{16}. Hence, the program cycles back to the first instruction. If we cycle through the program again we will store a 2_{10} in memory location 81_{16}. After checking to see that it is less than 101_{10}, this will be added to the number stored in memory location 82_{16} ($2_{10} + 1_{10} = 3_{10}$).

If you cycle through the program several times, the following will be observed. At each cycle we will add 1, 2, 3, ... to the sum. The accumulated sum will be stored in memory location 82_{16}. Prior to adding a number, that number will be stored in memory location 81_{16}. Before the addition is performed, this number will be subtracted from $65_{16} = 101_{10}$. (The 2's complement will be used here.) When the result of this subtraction is zero, computation stops.

Suppose that we want to change the program so that the sum $1 + 2 + \ldots + N$ is obtained. We need only to change the number stored in memory location 80_{16} from 101_{10} to $N + 1_{10}$.

Before considering the details of writing a program, we must understand its basic idea, called its *algorithm*. For instance, we

The Digital Computer

could express the idea of the program we have just considered in the following way. We want to obtain a result called SUM. Suppose that there is another number that we call N. Then, at the start, both SUM and N are made 0. Next, we add 1 to N. This number is tested to see if it is less than 101_{10}. If it is, then N is added to SUM and the process is repeated. On the other hand, if N is equal to 101_{10}, then the process stops and the value of SUM is the desired one.

The ideas of a program can be represented by a picture called a *flow chart*. Usually, such a picture is more easily understood than a verbal description. For instance, a flow chart for the program we have just discussed is shown in Fig. 6-6. Notice how the picture describes the operation of the algorithm. The diamond shaped block is used when a decision must be made (that is, there is conditional branching). If $N - 101 = 0$, then we "leave" the decision block along the branch marked "yes" and computation stops. On the other hand, if $N - 101$ is not equal to 0, then we leave the decision block along the branch marked "no" and N is increased by 1 and the operation is repeated.

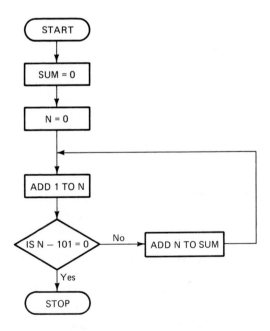

Fig. 6-6. A flowchart for the algorithm that adds $1 + 2 + \cdots + 99 + 100$

Output of Data

We now consider how data can be output by our simple program. Each input/output device is connected to a circuit called an *interface board* which, in turn, is connected to the bus. The interface board converts the digital information on the bus to information which can be used by the input/output device (and vice versa). Each input/output device generally has its own interface board but sometimes a single board is used by several devices. Memories called buffers, associated with input/output devices, are used to store the data sent or received. In some computers, the buffers are part of the main memory. The bus runs to all the interface boards, each of which is connected to its respective input/output devices. The input/output devices, such as terminals, graph plotters, tape drives, and line printers, are also called *peripherals*.

Let us assume that, in our simple computer, all data to be output is placed in the accumulator and then, on a suitable command, supplied to those leads of the bus reserved for input/output. To do this, let us use the machine language command:

$$00110000_2 = 30_{16} \qquad (6\text{-}8)$$

The command 30_{16} only specifies that data is to be output. The instruction must also indicate which device is to be used, and what function the device is to perform. For instance, suppose that a tape drive is employed. Information is often stored on tape in groups of data called "blocks." We could command the tape drive to wind the tape to the start of the first block. In this case, the data would be written over the first block. Alternatively, we could command the tape drive to skip over a block of data so that the new information would be written *after* the first block of data.

There are 16 bits in an instruction. If we want it to be an output instruction, then its form should be:

$$00110000 d_3 d_2 d_1 d_0 f_3 f_2 f_1 f_0 \qquad (6\text{-}9)$$

The 00110000 indicates that this is an output instruction. The d's and f's are additional bits. The d's indicate the device to be used for the output, and the f's would indicate whether or not the first block of data would be skipped. Let us use the following code for the devices:

$$0000_2 = 0_{16} \text{ terminal}$$
$$0001_2 = 1_{16} \text{ line printer}$$

$0010_2 = 2_{16}$ floppy disk drive

$0011_2 = 3_{16}$ tape drive

Consider some device functions. For the tape drive, we have:

$0001_2 = 1_{16}$ rewind tape to start

$0010_2 = 2_{16}$ skip to next block of tape

If the data were to be printed on the terminal, the command given would be:

$$0011000000000000_2 = 3000_{16}$$

The last three bits have no significance here and would be ignored. Or suppose that we want to put the output on magnetic tape and that we want to start the tape at the beginning and write over any material on the tape. Then, the command would be:

$$0011000000110001_2 = 3031_{16}$$

On the other hand, if we want to skip over the first block of data that is stored on the tape and write the new data after it, the instruction would be:

$$0011000000110010_2 = 3032_{16}$$

There would be similar commands for the floppy disk drive. For instance, the track to be recorded on could be specified.

All of the I/O interfaces are connected to the same bus leads. There is a decoder similar to the instruction decoder in Fig. 6-3, which causes the appropriate device interface to be activated and to operate in the proper way. The decoder receives the bits of (6-9):

$$d_3 d_2 d_1 d_0 f_3 f_2 f_1 f_0 \qquad (6\text{-}10)$$

It then sends an instruction signal to the appropriate interface so that the correct I/O device operates and inputs or outputs the data in the correct way.

When data is output, first an instruction such as (6-9) is put out on the I/O lines of the bus. Next, the numerical data is supplied on the same bus leads. Note that these numbers are supplied in *sequence*. Suppose that, in our simple computer, there is an instruction which causes the contents of the accumulator to be supplied to the input/output lines of the bus. Suppose that this instruction is:

$$01110000_2 = 70_{16}$$

First we would put the instruction (6-9) into the accumulator, then the instruction 70_{16} would be given. After this, the data to be output would be put in the accumulator and the command 70_{16} would be given again. For instance, suppose that we want to print the number that is stored in memory location 91_{16} on the terminal, and, in addition, store the number

$$0011000000000000_2 = 3000_{16}$$

in memory location 26_{16}. (Note that this is the command to operate the terminal.) Then, to output the data we would execute the following instructions (given in hexadecimal):

$$0200$$
$$0126$$
$$7000$$
$$0200$$
$$0191$$
$$7000$$

First we clear the accumulator, then add the contents of memory location 26_{16} to it. That puts the terminal command in the accumulator. The next instruction (7000_{16}) causes this to output on the input/output lines of the bus. The accumulator is then cleared and then the numerical data is added to it. Since the accumlator was first cleared, the data is now stored in it. Next, this number is supplied to the input/output lines of the bus. Note that the procedures for output of data often vary greatly from computer to computer and we shall discuss another procedure in Sec. 7-1. An understanding of the procedure in this section, however, should enable you to understand the procedures for all computers. In your computer the *details* of input and output instructions may be different from those we have discussed here. However, the basic *ideas* will be the same.

Input/output devices are slower than the computer's operation. It is very possible that data can be supplied at a faster rate than it can be printed. The input/output buffer (Sec. 6-4) relieves this problem. However, if data is supplied fast enough, the buffer can be filled. The input/output unit often has a one bit register called a *flag*. If the buffer is full, the flag is 0; if it is not full and can receive data, the flag is 1. When the flag is 0, it acts as a signal to the control unit and computation pauses. Data output continues, however. Once the input/output register can receive more data, the flag becomes 1 and computation proceeds.

Some computers have similar flags called input/output *interrupts*. These cause computation to pause if some predictable problems occur with an input/output device. If the line printer is out of paper, for example, computation will pause.

We can write statements in programs which call for input of data at specified times. In such cases, the data is put into the output register from one of the printers such as the terminal. When the appropriate command is given, it is input into the accumulator. Thus, data can be typed in when required. This input of data is much simpler than toggling in the program. We shall discuss simple procedures for input of programs in a subsequent section.

6-6. ASSEMBLY LANGUAGE

Programming using machine language is very tedious. The programmer must either remember the machine language codes such as those in Table 6-2 that correspond to each instruction or be continually obliged to look them up. In large computers, there may be many more instructions than are given in Table 6-2. This makes the job of using them all the more difficult. Another problem with machine language is that the programmer must remember the numerical addresses of all the memory locations used to store the variables as well as the memory locations of the commands involved in branching. As an example of some of these problems, suppose that we want to add the following:

$$x = a + b + c + d \tag{6-11}$$

There must be a memory location reserved for x, a, b, c, and d, and the numerical values of these locations must be remembered. If there are only a few variables, the task is relatively simple. However, in a large program, with many variables, the programmer must make a table which can be rather time-consuming.

In order to make programming less tedious, other types of languages have been developed for the programmer to use instead of machine language. In this section we shall discuss an *assembly language*. This is a language which is closely related to machine language, but is much easier for programmers to use.

Whenever a computer performs computations, a machine language *always* directs its operation. Consequently, whenever another form of language is used, it must be translated into machine language. A program called an *assembler* directs the computer to translate the assembly language program into machine language.

The assembly language is a set of instructions used to write an assembly language program. We shall first describe a simple assembly language and then talk about how the computer uses it.

The instructions in machine language are in terms of binary codes. In assembly language, these codes are replaced by *mnemonics*, easy-to-remember sequences of letters. For instance, instead of writing $01_{16} = 00000001_2$ for "add," we would simply write the letters ADD. Note that ADD is much simpler to remember than 00000001. We assume here that letters can be input to the computer. Of course, this cannot be done by toggling unless special codes are used.

We shall now present a simple assembly language. Note that, like machine languages, assembly languages are not standard. We shall use three letters to designate the assembly language instructions. It is often convenient to use a fixed number of letters for the assembly language instructions, but this is not always done. In general, each assembly language instruction will correspond to a machine language instruction.

Table 6-5: A Simple Assembly Language which Corresponds to the Machine Language of Table 6-2.

Machine language instruction in hexadecimal	Assembly language
01	ADD
02	CLE
03	AND
04	ORR
05	XOR
06	SHR
07	SHL
10	COM
11	INC
12	NEC
13	ZEC
14	PIM
20	BRU
21	BRZ
22	BRN
70	CON
77	STP

The Digital Computer

Note that the assembly language mnemonics are much easier to remember than the binary codes which they represent.

Another advantage of using an assembly language is that the programmer does not have to remember the memory locations of the stored or computed data. These values are called *variables* and can be given names. Usually, a name can consist of up to six alphanumeric characters.

To give an example of an assembly language program, let us rewrite the machine language program of Table 6-1 in assembly language.

Table 6-6: An Elementary Assembly Language Program

> CLE
> ADD DATA1
> ADD B
> PIM ANS
> STP
> DATA1:3
> B:4
> ANS:0

DATA1, B, and ANS are names of variables. DATA1 is equivalent to the specific memory location 10_{16} in Table 6-1. Similarly, B is written instead of specifying memory location 11_{16}, and ANS is written instead of specifying memory location 12_{16}. The programmer does not have to remember the memory locations. Any time that DATA1 is referenced, the correct memory location will be addressed.

Now let us see how the computer works with an assembly language program. A program called an *assembler* is written. This program is written only once and most programmers need not be concerned with it. The assembler program is then loaded into the memory in the same way that any program would be. The assembly language program is then input as *data*. The assembler translates the assembly language program into a machine language program, and this program is then entered and run in the same way that any machine language program would be. However, the programmer did not have to write it in machine language. Only the assembly language program had to be written.

The following procedure could also be used. The assembler translates the assembly language program into a machine language program which is stored in the memory. This program can then be output onto magnetic tape. Next, the memory is cleared and the assembled machine language program is input from the magnetic tape. Now the desired machine language program can be run. Again, note that the programmer did not have to write this program in machine language.

Let us see how the assembler program works. Remember that each statement of the assembly language program is input as data. If a terminal is used, each letter will generate a code (Sec. 4-6); thus, each instruction of the assembly language can be represented by a different sequence of 0's and 1's. When the assembler is put in the computer, each code is stored in a separate memory location. Similarly, the machine language codes which correspond to the assembly language codes are each stored in a memory location. Now, when a statement of the assembly language program is input, its code is compared with the stored assembly language codes. When a stored code is found to be equal to the input instruction code, the corresponding machine language instruction can be added to the machine language program that is being generated. The logic AND (Sec. 5-6) can be used here to make a comparison.

Now let us see how memory locations are allocated for variables. All variables used in an assembly language will always appear in the program following an instruction. Thus, alphanumeric information following the three letters of an instruction can be identified as a variable.

Now we shall talk about the actual formation of a machine language program from an assembly language program. The assembly language program is entered twice. (In some computers, it need only be entered once, but it is stored and *scanned* twice.) The first pass is used to identify all the variables and set up memory locations for them. The program is scanned, and the first time that a variable is encountered, its code is stored. The variable name (code) used is stored in a *symbol table.* This symbol table will eventually contain a memory location(s) for each variable. A variable may show up many times in the program, but it only appears once in the symbol table.

There must be memory locations assigned for each variable and for each instruction. On the first scan, a memory location is reserved for each instruction; memory locations for the variables are reserved after the memory locations for the instructions are reserved. Let's consider this by working with the program in Table 6-6. The first instruction is CLE. A word of memory was reserved for it. The memory locations will be assigned in order. The first instruction will be given the lowest memory number, for example,

$00000001_2 = 01_{16}$. Next, ADD DATA1 is encountered. A memory location (02_{16}) is reserved for ADD. DATA1 is entered into the symbol table but a memory location is *not* as yet reserved for it. Similarly, when ADD B is encountered, a memory location (03_{16}) is reserved for ADD and B enters into the symbol table. Similarly, PIM will have a memory location (04_{16}) reserved and ANS will be entered in the symbol table. When STP is encountered, a memory location (05_{16}) is reserved for it. Now DATA1:3 is encountered. The colon indicates that DATA1 is a variable. *Now* memory location (06_{16}) is assigned to it. This is entered into the symbol table corresponding to DATA1. Next a memory location (07_{16}) is reserved for B. Finally, when the last statement is encountered, a memory location (08_{16}) is reserved for ANS.

Data is identified by the colon (:). Its appearance indicates that the number following the colon is to be stored in the appropriate memory location. Note that there must be a data statement corresponding to each variable. (This may not be true for all assemblers.) For instance, after the sum was taken, we put the result in a memory location called ANS. We are requred to have a data statement which contains ANS. In Table 6-6, we had

ANS:0

This was necessary so that a memory location could be reserved for ANS. Note that the data value 0 is arbitrary. Any value could be used. After ANS is put in the memory, this value will be written over. We have assumed that memory locations are assigned in order, starting with 01_{16}. Some assemblers vary this procedure.

Now let's discuss the second pass. In the first pass, all of the memory locations were reserved. In the second pass, the mnemonic codes are converted into the machine language codes and stored in the assigned memory locations. This is the first part of the machine language word. If a variable name is associated with an instruction, then it is "looked up" in the symbol table; this memory location then becomes the second part of the machine language word. In this way, the complete machine language word is generated. This process is repeated step by step until the entire program is converted into machine language. Note that the instructions will be stored in sequence.

After the run of the assembler program is completed, the assembled machine language program, which is now stored in the memory, is usually output onto tape or punched cards. The memory is cleared and the machine language program can be run.

The memory may not be large enough to store the assembler, symbol table, plus the complete assembled machine language program. But, if the memory is large enough to complete pass 1, then the following can be done. Pass 2 is started. If the memory becomes full, then pass 2 pauses. The contents of the memory containing that part of the machine language program that has been assembled is output on tape or disk. After this is done, the part of the memory that stored the assembled program is cleared and pass 2 is resumed. The machine languge instructions of the assembled program that are generated can now be stored in the newly emptied memory locations. If the memory again becomes filled, pass 2 again pauses and the process is repeated.

6-7. LOADERS

When we discussed a machine language program in Sec. 6-5, we assumed that the program was toggled in. This is an extremely tedious way of entering data. It would be much simpler to type the program on a terminal. In Sec. 6-5 we learned that data could be entered in response to instructions in the program. There are machine language programs called *loaders* which enable us to enter programs as data. In such cases, terminals and other input/output devices can be used to input the data. For example, if we would want to run a program many times, the program could be stored on a floppy disk, and each time that it was needed, it could be input from the disk.

Let us discuss some elementary ideas about loaders. Suppose that we want to input a machine language program and have each instruction stored in a separate memory location. These are to be numbered consecutively. Let us start with 10_{16}. The loader program has an instruction in it to receive data. In response to this, one line of the program you are entering is typed in. This is stored in the ALU. The command 1490_{16} is given in our elementary machine language, and this causes the instruction to be stored in memory location 90_{16}.

When the next instruction is input, we want to store it in location 11_{16}. Thus, we want to change the loader program instruction 1490_{16} to 1491_{16}. Suppose that the instruction 1490_{16} is stored in memory location 10_{16}. We could put this number in the accumulator, increment it by one, and then put the new number 1491_{16} back into memory location 10_{16}. The next time that the instruction in memory location 10_{16} is executed, the contents of the accumulator will be stored in memory location 91_{16}. Proceeding in this way we can store the input instructions in successive memory locations.

Now let us see how we input the program. We shall assume that the input is from the terminal. The input word consists of a sequence of 0's and 1's. If this is the first word, then it will be stored in memory location 90_{16}. The loader program cycles again and the next input word is stored in memory location 91_{16}. In this way, the entire program is input and stored in memory locations 90_{16}, 91_{16}, 92_{16}, ... Then, the loader program is removed from the memory and the program is run. Note that, in order to run this program, we must start the program counter (PC) at 90_{16}. Usually, there is provision to do this.

We have greatly oversimplified loaders here. The loader can be a very complex program. Consider entering data on a terminal. A line of the program is typed. At the end of the line, a symbol is typed to indicate that the line is finished. Usually, this is a carriage return or a line feed. (These are separate buttons on a terminal.) The next line is typed followed by the line feed. This procedure is followed until the complete program is entered. Thus, the loader program must store each line of the program, and the memory locations must be assigned in order. The loader must be able to recognize the end of line symbol such as a carriage return. In addition, loaders may do more. On a terminal, when you finish typing a line, you must type a line feed to advance the paper and a carriage return which advances the carriage to the start of the line. It is troublesome for programmers to have to type both symbols; in some loaders, when a carriage return is typed, the loader program causes a line feed to be output to the terminal, thus saving the programmer work. The code output by the terminal may also be translated by the loader. For instance, the terminal output for a 1 is not just a 1 but a sequence of 0's and 1's. The loader could translate this into a 1.

A loader program can also be written so that the computer can accept data from many peripherals such as terminals, card readers, tape readers, and floppy disks. The loader program may be very long. Thus, it would be extremely tedious to toggle in. It would be much easier to enter the loader on the terminal or to store it on a floppy disk and enter it using the disk reader.

There is a procedure called *bootstrapping* that facilitates programming. (The name *bootstrapping* comes from the phrase "to pull yourself up by your own bootstraps.") A very elementary loader program is normally written and entered using toggling. This simple loader system may only allow you to enter data from a terminal in a very basic way. When a more complex loader is entered from the terminal, the first loader is removed from the computer, and the more complex loader program is run. This may permit data from a disk to be entered. The complete loader, which is now stored on the disk, can be entered and run.

There is another procedure that is commonly used which is also convenient. A loader is stored in a read only memory, which is actually part of the main RAM of the computer. This permits the complete loader to be used whenever it is desired.

6-8. HIGHER LEVEL LANGUAGES

Although assembly language is easier to use than machine language, it is still tedious. For instance, suppose that we want to write a program that evaluates the simple equation:

$$x = (a + b)(c - d)/(a - b) \qquad (6\text{-}12)$$

Many assembly language or machine language statements (lines) would have to be written. This would involve a great deal of work for the programmer. However, there are higher level languages such as BASIC, FORTRAN, and COBOL where this is not the case. For example, in one of these languages (BASIC), a program that would execute Eq. (6-12) for a = 3, b = 4, c = 5, d = 1.3 (all in base 10) is:

```
10  LET A=3
20  LET B=4
30  LET C=5
40  LET D=1.3
50  LET X=(A+B)*(C-D)/(A-B)
60  PRINT X
70  END
```

Note that * is the computer symbol for multiplication.

The program that actually runs the computer is in machine language. When a higher level language is used, the program is entered as data just as in the case of assembly language, and a machine language program is generated. The program that converts the higher level language program to machine language is much more complex than the assembler since a single instruction in a higher level language results in a *sequence* of machine language instructions. The programs that convert higher level languages into machine language are called *compilers* or *interpreters*. Even in higher level languages, there are very stringent rules that programmers must follow. However, higher level languages are much easier to use than assembly or machine languages.

EXERCISES

6-1. Describe the general organization of a digital computer.

6-2. What is the function of the control unit?

6-3. What is the function of a central processing unit?

6-4. Discuss various forms of input/output devices.

6-5. What is a microprocessor?

6-6. Discuss the function and makeup of the computer bus.

6-7. What is the function of the memory address register (MAR)?

6-8. What is the function of the memory buffer register (MBR)?

6-9. Describe the structure of the word in Fig. 6-2.

6-10. A memory has 32,768 words. How many bits must be used in the address field of a machine language word?

6-11. Write a simple machine language program that will perform $6 + 3 + 9$ and store the answer in a memory location. Use the machine language instructions in Sec. 6-3.

6-12. What are the functions of the fetch-execute register (FER) and the program counter (PC)?

6-13. Describe how a control signal decoder works.

6-14. Describe the functions of all the parts of the control unit in Fig. 6-4.

6-15. Describe the functions of all the parts of the memory unit in Fig. 6-4.

6-16. Describe the functions of all the parts of the central processing unit in Fig. 6-4.

6-17. Discuss the functions of all the parts of the input/output unit in Fig. 6-4.

6-18. Assume that N_1, N_2, and N_3 are three numbers that are stored in memory locations 91_{16}, 92_{16}, and 93_{16}, respectively. Write a program that adds $N_1 + N_2$. If the sum is less than 25, N_3 is subtracted from the result. If the sum of $N_1 + N_2$ is 25, computation stops. If the sum $N_1 + N_2$ is greater than 25, $2N_3$ is added to the result. The answer is to be stored in memory location 94_{16}.

Write the program with the following values for N_1, N_2, and N_3.

$$N_1 = 5$$
$$N_2 = 7$$
$$N_3 = 15$$

6-19. Write a machine language program that takes the sum

$$1 + 3 + 5 + 7 + 9 + \cdots + 99$$

6-20. Write a machine language program that performs the following:

$$1 - 3 + 5 - 7 + 9 - 11 + \cdots + 25$$

6-21. Discuss the input and output of data in terms of machine language instructions.

6-22. Write the program in Exercise 6-18 in assembly language.

6-23. Write the program in Exercise 6-19 in assembly language.

6-24. Write the program in Exercise 6-20 in assembly language.

6-25. Describe the function of a loader.

6-26. What is meant by "bootstrapping" loaders?

6-27. Discuss the differences among machine language, assembly language, and higher level languages.

6-28. What is the difference between an assembler and a compiler?

7 Computer Applications

In the past, computers were large and expensive, used mainly by large companies and universities. The first computers were used to solve extremely complex mathematical problems that would take days or years to perform if done by hand. As computers became cheaper, simpler programs were devised and run. Large companies started to use computers to keep records, make up payrolls, maintain inventories, and automatically reorder supplies.

As both the expense and size of computers were minimized, computers became readily available to individuals as well as to small businesses. In this chapter we shall consider the applications of these smaller computers in detail, and some of the limitations imposed upon them.

7-1. COMPARISON OF COMPUTERS

A small, complete computer "system" can be purchased for about $1000. A large computer system, in comparison, may cost many millions of dollars. In this chapter we discuss the differences among the various types of computer systems from the user's point of view.

There are various ways in which computers can be compared. Some of these are memory size, word size, speed, convenience of peripherals, and available software. Let us consider each of these.

Memory Size

The size of the memory determines the size of the programs that can be run on a computer. In general, the larger the size of the memory, the larger the program that can be stored. In addition, some programs require a great deal of storage space for data.

The number of words in the memory is usually a power of 2. For example, there may be 512 (2^9) words in a small memory, 4096 (2^{12}) words in a somewhat larger memory, 32,768 (2^{15}) words in a medium size memory, and many more in a larger memory. A memory with 4096 words is said to have 4000 or 4K (K = 1000) words. Similarly, a memory with 32,768 words is said to have 32K (or 33K) words.

Suppose that you want to program in the BASIC programming language. A BASIC compiler or interpreter must be used and the memory must be large enough to store it. There are many varieties of BASIC, the more powerful versions have many instructions and are very convenient to use. The simple versions have fewer instructions and are less convenient to use. In general, the more complex a language becomes, the more complex its compiler will be. Complex compilers afford certain advantages. Programmers, for example, often make mistakes when entering their programs. A complex compiler will cause the computer to send error messages that enable the programmer to easily locate some of the errors. For instance, the compiler may inform the programmer that there is an error in line number 20 of his program and the type of error may be indicated. A simple compiler may send a message saying only that the program will not run. If one has a long program to run, good error diagnostics can be very helpful and are almost a necessity.

The largest BASIC interpreter requires many words of memory (70K or more). However, there are very good BASIC interpreters which are designed for small computers that only require 12K words of memory. If your computer has only 8K, then this interpreter cannot be used. There are various other versions of BASIC that require 2K, 4K, and 8K words for their interpreter. The 2K version is very simple and, of course, only used on the smallest computers. Remember that the memory not only has to store the interpreter, but it must also store the BASIC program and the complete machine language program. Actually, not all of the complete machine language program has to be stored. It is possible to work with blocks of the program as discussed in Sec. 6-7 in conjunction with loaders.

There are other elements that occupy memory space. For example, in Sec. 6-4 we learned that there often is a buffer memory associated with the input/output devices. In small computers, this is often a part of the main memory. You have to be careful that you do not use an area of memory reserved for a buffer for other uses. Computer users often lay out memory maps that show them the allocation of the memory space. Locations $200_{16} - 300_{16}$, for example, could be reserved for an input/output memory buffer for the terminal. Such allocations make programming for input/output simpler. A more elaborate scheme for programs for input/output was presented in Sec. 6-5. If specific areas of memory are allocated to a specific input/output buffer, words can be read out of the memory in a predetermined order. This eliminates the need for much of the programming discussed earlier.

Another program that can be used is a text editor which enables you to easily enter a program and then correct it. Text editors can be very versatile. You can enter any text, including a program, search for a given string of characters anywhere in the text, change them or have surrounding text printed out. Sophisticated text editors can justify the output so that the printed copy has straight right and left margins. A new word-processing industry has developed using very sophisticated text editors.

A highly desirable system would have all of these helpful programs such as editors, loaders, and compilers stored on magnetic tape or disks. When we need them, simple commands from the terminal would cause the desired program to be loaded into the memory. In order to do this, a program called a *monitor* would have to stay in the memory at all times. The monitor directs the operation of the computer. Suppose that you want to run a BASIC program. The monitor would direct the loading of the BASIC interpreter into the memory, and the program would be interpreted and run. All of this is done with just a few commands from the user. (Of course, the BASIC program must be entered by the programmer.) Although monitors can make life easier for the programmer, they do take up memory space, and thus, there may be tradeoff between convenience and memory size.

The cost of the memory is a substantial part of the cost of a complete small computer. Most small computers have enough address lines to handle 32K or 64K words of memory. It is not necessary to purchase all this memory at the start. If you are purchasing a computer, you can start small and then work yourself up to a larger memory. The memory device paralleling technique discussed in Sec. 4-2 is used here.

Memories can also contain ROMs that can be used for many applications. Probably the most useful ROM that you can start with is one that contains a loader. This can relieve much tedium. However, ROMs can also be programmed to contain simple (or complex) programs, and as more and more sophisticated ROMs become available, the versatility of computers will increase.

PROMs can be used to store programs that are written by you and run often. For instance, you may develop an editor that you want to place permanently in storage. A PROM can be used for this purpose. Note that there must be sufficient address lines for all of the RAMs including the ROMs.

Remember that when a program is run, the memory must be able to store the complete machine language program and all the data. In certain programs, the amount of storage needed for this is very large. Such programs cannot be run on small computers.

Word Size

The size of the words used by the computer is related to the memory operation. In Sec. 5-5 we learned that 32 bits were needed to store a floating point number with relatively high precision. Suppose that each word of your computer is only 16 bits. If you want high precision, two words would be required to store each number. More complex programs would have to be written to allow the use of these words. For instance, in order to add two numbers, we would have to work with four words. Hence, with short words, we need more space to store some programs since they are made more complex due to the short word size. In addition, we need twice as many words to store the data. Short word size may also reduce the speed of the computer. For instance, if each number must be stored in two memory locations, then there must be two memory read cycles each time that we want to read a single number, which increases the computation time.

Actually, even with relatively large word size, we sometimes need to use two words to store each item of data. This is called *double precision*.

There are some special purpose computers that have only one-bit words. Small general purpose computers often have 8 or 16 bit words whereas large computers may have 32 or 64 bit words. Word size, just as memory size, limits the versatility and speed of the computer. If you intend to do extensive numerical calculations (rapidly), then a large wordsize, large memory computer may be necessary. However, there are very many useful and interesting programs that can be run on smaller wordsize computers, some of which we shall discuss. For these applications, the small wordsize is not a disadvantage.

Speed

The speed of computation varies greatly from one computer to another. Speed refers to the average time it takes for a computer to perform an operation. An estimate of the speed of computers can be obtained by comparing the frequencies of their master clocks. In general, the large, powerful computers are much faster than the smaller ones. In a typical case, a calculation on a medium speed, large computer might take five minutes while the same calculation performed on a programmable calculator might take five hours. A programmable calculator can be regarded as the simplest of the small computers. Again, this does not mean that small computers will always take an extremely long time to run their programs. There are many programs that run extremely fast on small computers. However, the large, high-speed machines will be significantly better when programs involving extensive calculations are run.

Convenience of Peripherals

The input/output devices are referred to as *peripherals*. These can make the job of programming a computer much easier. It is much simpler, for example, to enter a program using a terminal than to toggle it in. (This assumes that you have the appropriate loader.)

In general, a printing terminal is slow. If you use a cathode ray tube (CRT) or video terminal, the information is presented on a television-like screen. This can output data at a much faster rate since the letters do not have to be typed. Many printing terminals can receive data at 110 bits per second. (One bit per second is called a *baud*.) There are other terminals that can receive data at 1.5 to 3 times this rate (150 and 300 baud). A fast video terminal can receive data at up to 9600 baud. But while this is very fast, it is much slower than the speed of a fast computer. Some simple video terminals do not contain a CRT display. Instead, they generate a television signal, in which case you can use your own TV set for the display. This saves money since most people have TV sets.

Some video terminals contain their own small computers, and are called *smart terminals*. These terminals can usually store and edit several pages of text. After the text is corrected, it can be transmitted to the computer automatically, a great help to the programmer.

Often, we want a printed (hard) copy. This can be obtained from printing terminals but this process is slow. The *line printer* is much faster. With line printers, an entire line is printed at a single time. Note that printing terminals are slower than line printers.

Some of the most convenient peripherals allow you to store a great deal of information in terms of either programs or data. When such information is needed, it can be entered into the main memory. Tape drives allow the user to economically store large quantities of data. However, as we noted in Sec. 4-5, they are slow. Small computers often use tape for such storage since not only is the tape inexpensive, but the tape reader/writer can be a simple cassette recorder. The simple cassettes have one disadvantage: they cannot be easily reversed.

Much faster data interchange can be obtained from magnetic disks (Sec. 4-5). In general, hard disks store more information than floppy disks, but the floppy disks are relatively inexpensive. In fact, floppy disks are fast becoming an extremely popular form of auxiliary memory used with small computers. Another form of storage can be obtained by punching paper tapes. Although such tape is inexpensive, the readers and punches are not. At one time, paper tape was the most common low cost storage. Paper tape is still widely used, but magnetic tape and floppy disks are fast replacing it in many applications. Bubble memories are also used for this type of storage.

If you do not have any auxiliary equipment, then the operation of the computer can be very cumbersome. For instance, you would have to toggle in a loader and compiler as well as every program that is to be run. The output in such cases would be in LED figures, shown one memory location at a time. The inclusion of the appropriate peripheral can make the job of the programmer much simpler. If you consider purchasing a computer, then the cost of peripherals should be included in the total cost.

Available Software

Software refers to computer programs. Some computer manufacturers furnish a great deal of software with their computers; others do not. For instance, programs can be furnished for loaders, editors, monitors, and compilers. If you have such programs which are written for *your particular computer's* machine language, then you have cleared a large hurdle. Suppose you want to run a BASIC program on your computer, but you do not have a BASIC interpreter. And even though you may know someone with a BASIC interpreter, if his computer's machine language is not the same as yours, then you will have to translate it into your machine language. This may involve more than just changing from one code to another, since one machine language may contain instructions that are not available in another machine language. For example, suppose that one computer has a hardware multiplier. The machine language for this computer would contain a single command for "multiply." In your computer, however, you may have to write a long sequence of commands to obtain multiplication. The form of the machine language commands can vary from computer to computer, making the job of translating a program from one machine language to another very difficult.

Some manufacturers supply software in addition to editors, loaders, compilers, and monitors. There may be software packages that can be used to solve simultaneous equations or other mathematical problems. If you are considering purchasing one of two computers, then the available software supplied by a manufacturer may be an important factor in your choice.

7-2. THINGS THAT CAN BE DONE WITH A COMPUTER

In this section we shall concentrate on the applications of small computers. The simplest, consisting merely of microprocessors with very small memories, are used for control applications. The more complex, which have larger memories and more extensive input/output devices, are used for "more conventional" computer applications.

Control Applications

Simple microprocessors are used for the control of systems. For example, we have mentioned the use of a computer to control the environment of a building. In this case, the system is the building whose interior environment is to be controlled. When a home is to be heated, a thermostat turns on the heat when the temperature drops below a certain level, and turns it off when the temperature rises to a certain level. It may appear as though this should stabilize the temperature. But problems can arise. The temperature may overshoot the mark. The sunlight could strike certain windows and not others so that some rooms will be hotter than others. The heating system should take these factors into account also. In addition, the heaters should be turned off before the desired temperature has been reached to avoid overshoot. However, this will depend upon the outside temperature and sunlight.

Now suppose that there are temperature sensors in each room of the house and light sensors located outside of the house at many points to monitor the sunlight. The temperature sensors usually produce a voltage which is proportional to the temperature. By means of devices called *analog-to-digital converters*, which convert these voltages to digital numbers, all the light and temperature information can be input to a microprocessor, and a program can be written that controls the main heating plant. If forced air heat is used, the program can be designed so that the computer will not only turn on the main heating system, but will also control individual rooms. For instance, if the sun is shining on one side, some rooms will be warmer than others. Dampers could be arranged so that the air blowers would move heat from the warm side of the house to the cold side.

The heaters would also be adjusted so that there would be no overshoot of temperature. This adjustment would depend upon the outside temperature. Thus, a more comfortable and more efficiently heated house would result. This computer could also be used for other types of control. There could be temperature sensors mounted in the freezer. If it became too warm, an alarm would sound. A sophisticated burglar alarm could also be controlled by the computer.

Another example of control is a computer-controlled fuel injection system in an automobile. Sensors can be used to determine speed, engine temperature, air temperature, accelerator position, and the angle of the car (whether it is going up or down a hill). This and other pertinent information are fed into the computer, which then controls the injection of gasoline into the engine. The system could be much more elaborate than the ones in common use. A car run by such a computer could operate much more efficiently. The automobile computer could also be used to control the heater and air conditioner to keep the passenger compartment comfortable. Or it could be used to give the driver an indication of the miles per gallon of gasoline.

Account Management

Large businesses have been using computers to keep track of their affairs. Now that computers can be purchased by individuals, these computers can be used in corresponding functions in the home. For instance, since deposits and checks can be entered into the memory, checking accounts can be balanced. A warning message can also be printed if your balance becomes too low. In a similar way, purchases and expenses can be stored and the computer can maintain your budget; a warning message could even be printed if you spend too much!

The computer can be used for record storage. Recipes can be stored on a floppy disk, and when you want to cook a particular dish, you enter the name of the recipe. It will then be read from the disk and printed on the terminal. All this can be done with a simple command. Similarly, the computer can be used to keep other kinds of records that you frequently use such as telephone numbers and zip codes.

If the computer has an editor program, then homework can be typed in, checked and corrected. A perfect copy can then be typed out. Note that you only have to enter the rough first copy and the corrections. The computer does the rest.

The computer can be programmed so that the schedule for a baseball league can be worked out; it can be written so that all the teams are of equal ability. In this case, people would have to make judgments about each player's fielding, hitting, and throwing ability and assign him a rating. These would be entered with the player's name. A program would have to be written which would compare the various ratings and then assign the players to teams.

Individual records can be kept in a small computer. A student can use it to keep track of his grades or a teacher can use it to make up the grades for a class. In the latter case, the students' grades on all tests would be entered, and the computer would then average them out and assign the grades based upon a suitable curve.

Games

Small computers are popularly used to play games. There is an almost unending round of computer games. Each day more appear. The first games played by computers were tic-tac-toe, chess, and checkers. The computer games were played in the same way as the standard ones except that one person played "against the computer." The concept has been extended to the newer games. One popular game is based on the old television series "Star Trek." Here, the player guides his starship through space and searches for Klingon space ships. Another popular space game called "Lunar Lander" involves landing a space ship on the moon. The program takes both the thrust of the rockets and the gravity of the moon into account. The number of these games is almost endless. A good source for many computer games and their programs written in BASIC is the book *What To Do After You Hit Return*, published by the People's Computer Company of Menlo Park, California.

The TV-type computer games using "joystick" controls are also very popular. Here, the output is a CRT terminal or a TV set. The joystick is a lever that sticks out of a box. The position of the joystick is "translated" to the computer using variable electrical resistances connected to the stick. The motion of the joystick then moves figures on the screen. There are one- and two-dimensional joysticks which can be used to move a figure on the CRT screen through a maze, or to play hockey, tennis, or similar games.

Educational activities can also be programmed into computers. For example, an arithmetic problem can be typed out by the computer; the student then solves the problem and types in the answer. If it is correct, the computer poses a new problem; if incorrect, the player is told that the answer is wrong and that he must try again.

This type of game can be played with subjects more complex than ordinary arithmetic. Entire courses of study can be taught. The computer types out information on the subject to be studied, and after reading it, the student takes a multiple choice test "given by" the computer. The computer asks questions and the student answers them; if the answers are wrong, the student must study further and then take a different test. Once the student passes the test, more advanced material is given and the process is repeated. Self-taught computer courses are both educational and entertaining.

Word Processing

Computers are used in conjunction with complex editor programs to form the backbone of the *word-processing* industry. When a book was printed before the era of computers, lead type was produced. Spaces were introduced into each line so that the right margin was justified. Complex materials such as equations and mathematical symbols had to be manually set into position. All this has changed. Usually using a video terminal, the material is typed in, and the computer program then justifies the material. Often, an entire word will not fit on a single line. The word is then split in two, using a hyphen. Some editor programs perform this hyphenation automatically. In other cases, some editors will pause and let the programmer make the decision as to where the hyphens should be placed. Even complex mathematical material can be positioned easily using such equipment. These programs also have provision for correction. Errors can be changed, and additional material can be entered or existing material deleted.

Since it does not look as good as printing, an ordinary printing terminal cannot be used for the output here. Often, the printing is done optically. Instead of a letter striking an inked ribbon, which strikes the page, the letters are projected onto a sheet of photographic paper. In this way, the size of the letter and its shape (type font) can be easily varied. This optical printer is controlled by the computer. Other typesetting systems use a variable type such as that provided by the IBM "Selectric" elements. This book, for example, was typeset by a computer-controlled typesetting system.

Small Business Applications

Just as large businesses use larger computers for their record keeping, payrolls and inventories, so too can the small business use a smaller computer. Since the smaller business does not have the quantity of information to handle, it can use a computer with a smaller memory and which, of course, will be slower than the large, high-speed computers used by very large companies.

In business applications, records are stored on magnetic tapes or disks. When computations are to be performed, or records are to be updated, the appropriate material is read into the main memory; after the computation is performed, the new data is then written back onto the tape or disk.

One problem should be considered here. Computers may function improperly at times. They are said to "crash" or to be "down." Such failures, while relatively rare, can be due to failure of some of the components of the computer or to a loss of electrical power. Sometimes there can be problems with a monitor program so that the computer functions properly most of the time but certain combinations of commands result in a "crash." For instance, an erroneous instruction may cause data to be written over instructions. If such failures occur while data is being written or read from a disk or tape, the data can be lost. Some of these losses can be catastrophic and a great deal of data may be lost. Problems can also arise to cause *all* the stored information to be lost. If a business has all its records on a disk, for example, and the data is lost, then all of the business's records are lost. For this reason, all important data (not just business data) should *not* be stored on a single disk or tape. There should always be additional backup storage. This could be on other disks or tapes, or on punched tape. In addition, backup data could consist of printed records.

Other Computer Applications

Although we have considered numerous applications of computers here, we have not been complete since a complete discussion of all computer applications would fill serveral books. But some of the possibilities described here should suggest others. The uses to which you can put a computer are limited only by your inventiveness. We hope that the ideas discussed here will stimulate your imagination.

EXERCISES

7-1. Discuss how the memory size of a computer is related to its operation.

7-2. Discuss the memory size needed by a BASIC compiler.

7-3. Discuss the uses of ROM.

7-4. Discuss how the word size of a computer is related to its operation.

7-5. Discuss how the appropriate peripherals can make computer operation easier.

7-6. Why should software be a consideration in the choice of a computer?

7-7. What are some computer applications in the area of control? Use original ideas.

7-8. Discuss the educational and recreational uses of the computer.

7-9. Discuss uses for a computer in your home.

7-10. Discuss the uses of a small business computer.

8 Available Small Computers

We devote this chapter to a discussion of small computers and the related components that can be purchased by individuals for their own use or by small businesses. Although we do not intend to present a catalogue of available equipment, we shall discuss some specific products. The market is changing so rapidly that such a catalogue would be incomplete before the book was printed. The objective here is to give you an idea of the types of equipment available and hope that this will enable you to evaluate all the equipment that is on the market as well as the new equipment that will be available for a time to come. Specifically, we shall discuss the various types of microprocessors, the basic computer, peripherals, and software. Mention will also be made of some teaching aids that are helpful in evaluating microprocessors.

8-1. MICROPROCESSORS

The microprocessor is the heart of the small computer. Since there are many microprocessors produced by a number of manufacturers, let us start by considering the ways in which these can be compared. We shall assume that you are familiar with the discussion in Sec. 7-1.

Word Size

Microprocessors are made in various word sizes. Typically, there are word lengths of 1, 4, 8, 12, and 16 bits. The small word size processors are used for control applications such as those discussed in the last chapter. The larger word size processors are used in small, general purpose computers or for those control applications that require very precise operation. The data in such cases is supplied with many significant figures which would probably require the use of the larger word size microprocessor. Typically, small computers use 8 or 16 bit microprocessors.

Machine Language

The machine language or *instruction sets* of different microprocessors vary greatly. For instance, one may have many instructions in its machine language, while another may have only a few. In general, all the instructions of a large machine language can be carried out using a simple machine language, but it will often require a sequence of commands to accomplish what can be done with just one command in the large machine language. Thus, programming with a small machine language can be tedious; the program also becomes much longer, thereby using more of the memory. But a large instruction set can increase the power of a computer by reducing the memory requirements.

There is another side to this story. Your particular applications may only require a simple machine language. In such cases, the size of the machine language would not enter into your choice of microprocessors.

Speed

As discussed in Sec. 7-1, the speed of operation is sometimes a prime consideration in the choice of a microprocessor. If a great number of computations are to be performed, then high speed operation is often necessary. On the other hand, there are many applications where very high speed is not necessary. But if high speed is of prime importance, then the entire computer should be fast, and not just the microprocessor. The memory should also be chosen for its speed.

Software Support

As pointed out in Sec. 7-1, manufacturers may supply the users of their products with either a great deal of software or none at all. This software support is often an extremely important criterion in the choice of a product.

Available Microprocessors

While there are very many microprocessors, we shall concentrate on those commonly used in small computers. A good reference that provides data sheets for all microprocessors is found in *Electronic Design* magazine, vol.25, no.21.

To begin our discussion of microprocessors commonly used in small computers, let us consider 8-bit word chips. A popular microprocessor chip that has been used in many computer systems is the 8080A or MCS 80, manufactured by INTEL Corporation. There are 78 instructions in its machine language. It has a maximum clock frequency of 3MHz (3×10^6 cycles per second). There are 16 memory address lines so that 65,536 words can be addressed. The software support includes an assembler, editor, and a high level language PL/M. In addition, there is a library of programs that users have developed which is maintained by INTEL Corporation.

An updated version of the 8080, called the 8085 or MCS-85, is also manufactured by INTEL. It has two more instructions and many of the peripheral circuits that are needed already built into the chip.

Another commonly used chip is the Z-80, manufactured by Zilog, Inc. This is also an updated version of the 8080. The Z-80 has 16 address lines, so that 65,536 words can be addressed. It has 158 machine language instructions. The maximum clock frequency of the Z-80 is 4.5 MHz. There is strong software supplied for the chip, including an assembler, editor, and several high level languages, including BASIC and a floppy disk support system. This is a very fast and powerful microprocessor.

Another widely used microprocessor is the MC6800, manufactured by Motorola Semiconductor Products. This has 72 machine language instructions and 16 memory address lines so that 65,536 words can be addressed. The maximum clock frequency is 2 MHz. there is strong software support for this chip, including an assembler, editor, and both BASIC and FORTRAN high level languages. In addition, a library of users' programs is maintained.

A popular microprocessor, which is commonly used for control application, is the SC/MP or the SC/MP II, commonly called the "SCAMP". They are manufactured by National Semiconductor. There are 46 instructions in their machine language and their maximum clock frequency is 1 MHz. There are 12 address lines so

4096 words can be addressed. The available software consists of an assembler and a special high level language.

The 2650 microprocessor manufactured by Signetics has 75 machine language instructions. There are 15 address lines so that 32,768 words can be addressed. The maximum clock frequency is 2 MHz. The software supplied consists of a ROM editor, a FORTRAN compiler and other high level languages.

We have not listed all the 8-bit processors here but have discussed representative ones. There are others, and new ones are being continuously developed.

Now consider some 16-bit microprocessors. The 9440 manufactured by Fairchild Camera and Instrument Corporation behaves externally like the CPU of the Nova minicomputer, manufactured by Data General Corporation. The software of the 9440 is comparable to the one developed for the Nova which has 120 instructions. The maximum clock frequency is 10 MHz. There are 15 address lines so that 32,768 words can be addressed. The software includes an assembler, editor, monitor, and high level languages, including BASIC and FORTRAN.

The MN601 manufactured by Data General Corporation has 72 instructions. There are 15 memory address lines so that 32,768 words can be addressed. The maximum clock frequency is 8.3 MHz. The software includes editors, a monitor, and higher level languages, including FORTRAN and BASIC.

The TMS-9900/SBP-9900 are manufactured by Texas Instruments, Inc. There are two different models which are fabricated using different types of integrated circuits. There are 69 instructions and 15 memory address lines so that 32,768 words can be addressed. The maximum clock frequency is 4 MHz. The available software includes an assembler, editor, and high level langauges, including BASIC and FORTRAN. A program library is also maintained.

Again, we have not listed all the available 16-bit microprocessors but have included a representative list. Remember that new chips are constantly being developed.

Learning Aids

Many manufacturers, as well as some independent companies, offer learning aids. These are intended to enable the user to learn about the microprocessor, its programming, and its potential applications. These aids are primarily designed for engineers who will use the microprocessor for various applications; some of the simpler ones, however, can be helpful to the beginner.

8-2. COMPLETE SMALL COMPUTERS

The complete computer system includes the microprocessor, memory, power supply, and input/output ports or interfaces. We shall first consider those parts that we have not previously discussed and then talk about some of the computers that are available. Again, we shall not present a complete catalogue but only mention some of the more popular computers. This should provide you with sufficient information to be able to evaluate the computer you are going to purchase.

The power supply converts the 110 volt 60 Hz power line voltage into direct voltage which is used by the computer circuits. This is usually 5 volts but can lie in the range of 5 to 15 volts. A good power supply will provide a direct voltage that is almost completely free of alternating components. In addition, it will be well *regulated*; that is, its voltage should not change with fluctuations in the supply line voltage or with the current supplied to the computer. The power supply should isolate the computer from "spikes" of voltage that appear on the power line and that can disturb the computer's operation. For example, such spikes can change stored 0's to 1's and vice versa. The power supply must be capable of supplying the necessary current not just to the computer itself, but to the other components such as peripherals (although some of these have their own power supply). There should be a reserve available so that you can expand the computer without having to purchase a new power supply.

The input/output ports enable you to connect or interface the computer with its peripherals. The simplest computers may not have provision for such interfacing. For instance, suppose that toggling data is used for input. Then, the front panel will contain a set of toggle switches. The output of such a very simple computer will consist of a set of LED display numbers. These were illustrated in Fig. 3-33. The contents of a single register or memory location can be be output using these LEDs. The output is ususally provided in hexadecimal or octal. Using a computer with this type of input and output is extremely cumbersome and, as discussed, the use of the appropriate peripherals can be a great help. Usually, appropriate circuitry can be added to the simple computer so that it can work with peripherals. This circuitry is contained on the input/output port or input/output board or interface board. (These are equivalent names.)

If a peripheral is to be used, there must be logic circuits, called *interface boards* or *input/output ports*, that appropriately decode the input/output instructions (see Sec. 6-5). In addition, the appropriate electrical contacts must be provided so that the peripheral can be connected to the computer. Sometimes, all of the necessary logic is incorporated in the computer; it is not commonly done, however, and input/output ports must be provided. A separate port is usually used for each peripheral.

Incidently, if a computer does not have toggle switches and LED output, then you can assume that it is to be connected to appropriate peripherals. On the other hand, even if it has toggles and LED displays, this does not mean that more convenient forms of input/output cannot be used.

Note that almost all small computers are expandable. For instance, additional memory can be added by plugging it into the bus. In a small computer, the bus (or at least part of it) consists of printed wiring on a printed circuit board. Connectors are provided so that additional memory or other equipment can be added to the computer. This printed circuit board, which holds most of the semiconductor circuitry of the computer, is called a *mother board*.

As we begin our discussion of available computers, remember that we are not presenting an exhaustive catalogue but merely a list of some representative systems. The Digital Equipment Corporation (DEC) LSI-11 microcomputer is a powerful computer system. It is backed up with extensive software that includes assemblers, loaders, a sophisticated monitor system, and high level language support, including **BASIC** and **FORTRAN**. Semiconductor and core RAM is also available. In addition to a large set of machine language instructions, DEC supplies an almost complete line of peripherals, including printing terminals, line printers, floppy and hard disks, magnetic tape drive, and paper tape drive. Simplified time-sharing can also be performed with this computer system. The DEC LSI-11 is probably too elaborate and expensive a system to be used by most hobbyists or individuals; it is well suited, however, to small businesses. Computer clubs might well consider this extensive system.

The Heathkit H-11 is a 16-bit word computer based upon the (DEC) LSI-11 CPU. It is currently one of the few computers in the personal computer price range that has 16-bit words. Its memory can be expanded to 32K words. There is very extensive software backup since DEC's software is available to H-11 users.

Available Small Computers

This includes editors, loaders, and the BASIC language. The Heathkit computer system makes considerable use of paper tape storage, although cassette and disk storage are also available. Video and printing terminals are provided as well.

The Altair 8800 family consists of computers which are widely used for small business applications and by computer hobbyists. The latest model in the series is the 8800B. While these computers provide toggle input, they are in no way limited to it. There is provision for interfacing to such peripherals as cassette tape, floppy disks, printer and video terminals, and line printers. The bus structure, consisting of 100 lines, was developed by MITS; it is de facto standard in hobby computing. It interfaces most easily with most small computer peripheral equipment, although it will not interface with all equipment directly. The back case of the computer has provision for easy connection to peripherals. The appropriate input/output ports must be added to accomplish this. The computer is based upon the 8080 chip or its "updated" version. Thus, it is an 8-bit word machine, and the memory is expandable up to 64Kwords.

The IMSAI 8080 is another machine which uses the 8080 microprocessor or one of its updated versions. It uses the Altair 100-lead bus and thus is compatible with peripheral ports which can use the Altair bus. The computer is provided with a very heavy duty power supply that can provide power to almost all peripherals that would be desired.

The Radio-Shack TRS-80 computer uses a Z-80 microprocessor. It, too, is based upon the original 8080 chip and has an 8-bit word with a memory which is expandable to 62K. There are numerous peripherals provided, including a video terminal and an interface usable with a simple cassette recorder. The BASIC language is also provided.

Another computer based upon the 8080 chip is the Heathkit H-8 computer. This is one of a pair of computers brought out by the Heath company. The other is larger, the H-11 discussed earlier. The H-8 has a smaller word size (8 bits). It has a LED front panel display. Instead of toggles, a push button keyboard is provided. Software is available, including the BASIC language. This computer offers paper tape as one of its primary memory elements. Other peripherals are available, including video terminals and tape storage.

The 8-bit machines we have discussed so far are based on the 8080 or Z-80 chips. There are a number of machines which are based upon the 6800 microprocessor. One of the most popular of these is the Southwest Technical Products SWTPC 6800 computer.

This is an 8-bit word machine. Its memory is expandable to 64K. SWTPC makes extensive use of ROMs. For instance, there is a monitor ROM and a BASIC ROM. Material is also provided on tape. SWTPC provides numerous peripherals, including video terminals, audio cassette interfaces, printers, and an interface with an ordinary TV set.

Most small computers are based upon a single microprocessor chip. An exception to this is the "system" of the Digital Group. Their philosophy is that microprocessors will improve and that a system based upon a single microprocessor will become obsolete. The microprocessor actually represents a very small fraction of the system's cost. By appropriate design of logic circuits, the memory and peripherals of the Digital Group are made relatively independent of the microprocessor type. In fact, the Digital Group computers can be modified to use the Z-80, 8080A, 6800, and 6501/6502 microprocessors. The Digital Group also supplies a full line of peripherals, including video terminals, cassette recorders, interfaces and line printers. Extensive software support is also provided.

We have briefly discussed a few computers. There are many more. If you intend to purchase a computer, then you must consider the jobs that the computer will be called upon to perform. This will give you some idea of the requirements on memory, word size, and speed. The future uses as well as the immediate ones should be considered. It is a poor investment to purchase a computer that will soon become obsolete. Individual users should seek out computer clubs where they can gain from the experience of others. There are also various computer stores that offer a wealth of information; they have computers that they can demonstrate for you. In addition, considerable reading material is generally available.

Several computer magazines oriented to individual users are *BYTE, Interface Age, Interface*, and *Kilobaud*. The latest computers will be advertised and discussed there, along with helpful articles on hardware and software. If you run some sample programs either at a computer store or at a club, these will be a great help in showing you the advantages and disadvantages of the system which you are considering.

8-3. PERIPHERALS

We have discussed how the use of peripherals can make the programming of a computer much less tedious. If complex programming is to be done, the appropriate peripherals are really a necessity. In this section we shall talk about various types of peripherals that are available, providing information which will hopefully enable you to make an intelligent choice when you purchase your own.

Terminals

We shall discuss input/output terminals first. By a terminal, we mean a device with a keyboard that can input and output data. The output is either produced as a hard copy (printed characters on a page) or as a video output. The original hard copy terminal was the Teletype, and terminals of this type are widely used today. The impression is made by metallic type striking an inked film which strikes the paper. Printing terminals of this type are made by Teletype Corporation, IBM and others. Another common type of printer uses no type; instead the printer produces an array of closely spaced dots. The terminal controls which dots are printed. This type of printing is very versatile since an almost unlimited set of characters can be produced by choosing which dots are printed. If high quality printed material is important, however, then the type faces produce better results. On the other hand, dot array material is very readable.

The speed of printing is important, as anyone who has waited for a long program or long list of data to be printed well knows. The slowest printing terminal will accept data at 110 baud (bits/second). There are faster ones that print at 2 to 4 times this speed. The fastest terminals are the video terminals. Here, a "page" of data is displayed on a television-like screen. The speed at which these terminals can operate also varies, the fastest ones operating at 9600 baud.

When terminals are operated, the signal must be supplied to it in the proper form. Each symbol is encoded as a sequence of 0's and 1's. For printing terminals, these usually must be supplied serially, one bit at at time. This was discussed in Sec. 3-8. When all the bits that specify a character are received, the terminal prints that character. This type of serial data transmission is slow. Some video terminals can receive all bits for a single character at once. This is parallel data transmission and is, of course, much faster.

Line Printers

When a great deal of hard copy is desired, the printing terminal is usually too slow. In such cases, a line printer can be used. In a printing terminal, each letter is printed separately, where a printing element prints a letter, then spaces to the next position and prints the next letter, and so forth. These can print at 8 to 16, or more, characters per second. However, they are still slow when a great deal of data is to be printed.

In the high speed line printer, there is a printing element for each character position so that a single line can be printed out at once. Thus, very rapid printing is possible.

Input/Output Boards-Interface Board

In order to operate a printing terminal or any other peripheral, the proper signals must be supplied. This requires logic circuitry to produce the appropriate 0's and 1's plus any other signal needed to operate the device. As we discussed in the last section, such circuitry is usually mounted on a board called an *input/output board* or an *interface* board. Usually, a board is designed to drive a particular device such as a printing terminal. However, there are several universal boards that can be used with many devices (often built by the manufacturer of the board). These are usually more expensive. Note that these boards are sometimes described in terms of series or parallel data transmission. The type of peripheral used, of course, determines the type of data transmission required.

Tape Storage

Large computers use special tape drives for their tape storage. These operate at very high speeds and can "wind through" a long tape very rapidly. Most small computers use much simpler tape drives which are, in fact, simple cassette recorders. Such recorders are designed to reproduce speech and music rather than 0's and 1's. The interface circuitry for these recorders takes this into account. It generates two tones, usually 2400 Hz and 1200 Hz. The 2400 Hz represents a 1, and the 1200 Hz represents a 0. During recording, the input sequence of 0's and 1's is translated into a sequence of 2400 Hz and 1200 Hz tones. Similarly, the interface board translates the 1200 Hz and 2400 Hz tones from the cassette recorder into 0's and 1's.

In general, when data is read from a recorder on a tape, the computer controls the tape drive. It may read a block of data, stop the tape, and then start it again and read or write additional data later. In complex systems, the tape may be rewound to the start of a block, and then the data can be read again or be written over. An ordinary cassette recorder can usually be stopped or started by remote control. The interface board has circuitry that accomplishes this. However, a simple cassette recorder cannot be reversed without the reverse button's being pushed. The computer cannot push the button. Thus, computer-controlled reverse cannot be obtained using simple tape cassette recorders. Cassette recorders that are designed for computer use have a remote controlled reverse.

Disk Storage

The fastest type of auxiliary magnetic storage commonly in use is disks. In Sec. 4-5 we described both the hard disk and floppy disk storage. In general, the hard disk storage is faster and will store much more data than the floppy disk. However, the floppy disk is much less expensive. Floppy disks are much faster than tape storage and will store a great deal of data. Any computer which is used extensively, such as a small business computer or even an individual's computer where many programs are run and speed is important, should have at least a floppy disk capability. Disk capability can be added to most computer systems. Thus, you can start with simple cassette storage and then add a floppy disk at a later time. You should make sure that this is possible before you purchase a computer.

Paper Tape

Another method of storage is on paper tape. Here, holes are punched in the tape, usually in accordance with the ASCII code (Sec. 4-6). Thus, alphanumeric data can easily be stored on paper tape. Paper tape readers and punches originally were supplied with Teletypes. They can now be obtained as stand-alone devices. There are both mechanical and optical paper tape readers. The optical tape readers are faster and, since they do not use mechanical fingers to sense the holes in the tape, they produce less wear and tear on the tape.

Modem-Telephone Coupler

The *modem* or *telephone coupler* is a device that allows you to connect a computer into a telephone system. (Modem is a combination of the words *modulator* and *demodulator*.) Using modems, you can supply information to a computer from a remote location. This is usually done when computers are timeshared. The modem is a rectangular box designed so that the telephone handset fits into it. The transmitter (mouthpiece) of the telephone is pressed against a small loudspeaker, and the receiver of the telephone (earpiece) is pressed against a small microphone. The modem translates 0's and 1's into audio tones. For instance, suppose that you have a terminal producing a sequence of 0's and 1's. This would be connected to a modem that would generate the appropriate audio tones. The loudspeaker of the modem would send these sounds to the transmitter of the telephone. These tones would be transmitted over the telephone lines. At the other end, the receiving telephone would also be placed in a modem. The tones from the telephone receiver would be picked up by the modem microphone and would be converted to 0's and 1's which are supplied to the computer. Thus, even though the terminal might be many miles away, the computer would function as if the terminal were connected directly.

EXERCISES

8-1. Discuss the various ways used to rate microprocessors.

8-2. Compare the various microprocessors discussed in Sec. 8-1.

8-3. List and discuss the functions of the parts of the small computer.

8-4. What criteria would you use if you were going to buy a small computer?

8-5. Compare the various computers discussed in Sec. 8-2.

8-6. Study the magazines devoted to small computers. List the computers given there and compare the different ones. The prices of the computers should be considered.

8-7. Consider the jobs/activities that you would like to perform with a computer. Then rate the computers in Exercise 8-5 and 8-6 in terms of these jobs.

8-8. Discuss the various peripherals that can be used with a computer.

8-9. Discuss the differences among the various kinds of terminals.

8-10. What are the differences among the various data storage peripherals?

8-11. What is the need for an input/output board?

8-12. How is data communicated to a computer from a remote point?

Index

Access time, 86
Account management,
 use of computer for, 168
Accumulator, 93, 113
Adder, 37
 full, 39
 half, 38
Addition, 112
Address, 66
Address decoder, 70
Algorithm, 146
Altair 8800 computer, 179
ALU, 5, 93, 113
AND, 27
Arithmetic:
 binary, 14, 19
 modular, 93, 97
 octal, 17
Arithmetic Logic Unit, 5,
 113
ASCII, 88
Assembler, 151, 153
Assembly language, 151
Assembly language program,
 153
Auxiliary memory, 5, 65,
 126

Back up storage, 171
Base, 9
 change of, 14
BASIC, 3, 158
Baud, 165
Binary arithmetic, 14, 19, 93, 97,
 106
Binary number system, 4, 9
Binary variable, 26
Bistable multivibrator, 43
Bit, 21
Block, 147, 182
Board:
 input/output, 182
 interface, 182
 mother, 128, 178
Bootstrapping, 157
Branch, 141
Bubble memory, 88, 166
Buffer, 139
Bus, 128
Byte, 110
BYTE, 180

Card punch, 6
Card reader, 6
Cassette recorder, 166, 183

Cell, memory, 67
Central processing unit, 5, 126
Check:
  negative, 120
  zero, 121
Chip enable line, 74
Chip select line, 73
Circuit:
  combinational, 27
  sequential, 43
CLEAR, 49, 116
Clock, 45, 126, 138
Clocked flip-flop, 45
  D, 47
  J-K, 47
  R-S, 44
  T, 49
Clocking, 45, 50
COBOL, 158
Code, 88
  ASCII, 88
  EBCDIC, 88
  error detecting, 90
Combinational circuit, 27
Compiler, 158
Complement, 30
Complete computer, 136
Computer, complete, 136, 177
  comparison of, 161
  organization of, 125
  personal, 3
Congruent, modulo, 98
Control, use of computer for, 167
Control unit, 5, 125, 138
Core, 5, 78
Counter, 58
CPU, 5, 126

CRT, 165
CU, 5, 138

D flip-flop, 47
Data, 153
Data General MN 601, 176
Decimal number system, 4
Decoders:
  address, 70
  instruction, 134
Dependent variable, 26
Destructive readout, 79
Digit:
  least significant, 21
  most significant, 21
Digital Equipment Corporation
  LSI-11 computer, 178
Digital Group, 180
Direct access memory, 86
Directory, 85
Disk, 166
  floppy, 87, 166, 183
  hard, 87, 183
  memory, 86, 183
Division, 106, 112
Double precision, 111, 164
Drive, LED, 60
Drum memory, 83, 87

EBCDIC code, 88
Edge-triggered flip-flop, 51
Editor, 164
Educational games, 170
8080A microprocessor, 175
Entering of instructions, 131
Equivalent, modulo, 98
Erase, 70
Erasable ROM, 82
Error, roundoff, 17, 112
Error detecting code, 90

Index

Exclusive OR, 32
Execution of instruction, 132
Exponent, 108

Fairchild 9440, 176
False, 25
FER, 135
Ferromagnetic, 83
Fetch-execute register, 135
File, 85
Flip-flop, 43
  clocked, 45
  D, 47
  edge-triggered, 51
  J-K, 47
  master-slave, 51
  R-S, 44
  T, 49
Floating point number, 108
  normalized, 109
  scaled, 109
Floppy disk, 87, 166, 183
FORTRAN, 158
Fractional part, 12, 108
Field, 130
Full adder, 39

Games, 169
  educational, 170
Gate, 27
  AND, 27
  exclusive OR, 32
  interconnection of, 34
  NAND, 32
  NOR, 31
  NOT, 30
  OR, 29
  XOR, 32
General organization of computer, 125

Half adder, 38
Hard copy, 127, 166
Hard disk, 87, 183
Hard wired multiplier, 107
Hardware, 100
Heathkit H-8 computer, 179
Heathkit H-11 computer, 178
Hexadecimal, 9
Higher level language, 158
Hysteresis loop, 76

IMSAT 8080, 179
Independent variable, 26
Information storage, 2
Inner memory, 65
Input:
  parallel, 52
  serial, 52
  series, 52
Input/output board, 178, 182
Input/output device, 6, 139, 181
Input/output interrupt, 151
Input/output port, 178
Instruction decoder, 134
Instruction register, 134
Instruction, execution of, 132
Instruction set, 174
Integrated circuits, 8
INTEL, 175
Interconnection of gates, 34
Interface, 180
Interface Age, 180
Interface board, 148, 178, 182
Interpreter, 158
Interrupt, 151
IR, 134

J-K flip-flop, 47
Joy stick, 170

Kilobaud, 180

Languages:
  assembly, 151
  BASIC, 158
  COBOL, 158
  FORTRAN, 158
  higher level, 158
  machine, 140, 174
Large scale integration, 8
LCD, 60
LCD driver, 60
Learning aid, microprocessor, 176
Least significant digit, 21
LED, 60
LED driver, 60
Light emitting diode, 60
Lines:
  chip enable, 74
  chip select, 73
  output enable, 74
  sense, 78
Line printer, 6, 166, 181
Liquid crystal display, 60
Loader, 156
Logic, 25
  mathematical, 25
Logic variable, 25
Logical notation, 25
Loop, hysteresis, 76
LSI, 8
"Lunar Lander", 169

Machine language, 140, 174
Machine language program, 130, 140, 174
Magnetic memory, 76
Main memory, 5, 65
Main memory unit, 5, 126

MAR, 129
Master clock, 138
Master-slave flip-flop, 51
Mathematical logic, 25
MC 6800 microprocessor, 175
Medium scale integration, 8
Memory, 43
  auxiliary, 5, 65, 126
  bubble, 88, 166
  direct access, 86
  disk, 83, 86, 183
  drum, 83, 87
  inner, 65
  magnetic, 76
  main, 5, 65
  nonvolatile, 65, 79
  paralleling of, 73
  random access, 66
  read only, 5, 65, 80
  semiconductor, 66
  sequential access, 66, 86
  size of, 161
  tape, 83, 166, 182
  volatile, 69, 79
Memory address register, 129
Memory buffer register, 129
Memory cell, 67
Memory unit, 5, 138
Microprocessor, 3, 8, 126, 173
  learning aids for, 176
MMU, 5, 126
MN 601 microprocessor, 176
Mnemonic, 152
Modem, 183
Modular arithmetic, 93, 97
Modulo, 58, 98
Most significant digit, 21
Mother board, 128, 178
Motorola MC 6800, 175
MSI, 8

Index

MU, 138
Multiplexer, 41
Multiplication, 106, 112
Multiplier, hard wired, 107
Multivibrator, bistable, 43

NAND, 32
National Semiconductor SC/MP, 175
Negative check, 120
Negative numbers, 103
9440 microprocessor, 176
9900 microprocessor, 176
Nondestructive readout, 70
Nonvolatile memory, 65, 79
NOR, 31
NOT, 30
NOVA, 176
Number, floating point, 108
Number system, 9
    binary, 4
    decimal, 4

Octal, 9
    arithmetic using, 18
One, 9, 25
Operational code, 130
OR, 29
Output, 148
Output device, 6, 181
Output enable line, 74
Output:
    parallel, 54
    serial, 54
Overflow, 21, 105

Paper tape, 6, 166, 183
Parallel input, 52
Parallel output, 54
Parallel to serial converter, 58

Paralleling of memory chips, 73
PC, 135
Peripheral, 148, 165, 180
    convenience of, 165
Personal computer, 3
Port, input/output, 178
Power supply, 177
Preset, 49
Printer, line, 166
Printing terminal, 6, 127, 165, 180
Program, 2
Program counter, 135
Programmable ROM, 82
PROM, 82

Radio Shack TRS-80, 179
Radix, 9
    change of, 14
RAM, 66, 80
Random access memory, 66
Read, 66
Read only memory, 5, 65, 80
    erasable, 80, 82
    programmable, 80, 82
    uses of, 180
Readout:
    destructive, 79
    nondestructive, 70
Read/write lead, 67
Record storage, 169
Register, 21, 52
    shift, 52
Regulation, 177
Relay, 7
Reset, 44
ROM, 5, 65, 80
    erasable, 80
    programmable, 80
    uses of, 180

Roundoff, 17, 112
R-S flip-flop, 44
   clocked, 45

Saturation, 76
Scaling, 109
SCAMP, 175
Scan, 154
Scanner, 127
SC/MP microprocessor, 175
Semiconductor memory, 66
Sense line, 78
Sequence detector, 61
Sequence generator, 61, 62
Sequential access memory,
   66, 86
Sequential circuit, 43
Serial input, 52
Serial output, 54
Serial to parallel converter,
   54
Series input, 52
Set, 44
Shift register, 52
Signetics 2650, 176
Size:
   memory, 161
   word, 164, 173
Small business applications,
   171
Smart terminal, 165
Software, 166
   supplied, 174
Speed, 165, 174
"Star Trek", 169
State, 43, 78
Storage, back up, 171
Subtraction, 112
Switch circuit, 36
Symbol table, 154

T flip-flop, 49
Table:
   symbol, 154
   truth, 26
Tape:
   magnetic, 83, 85, 166, 182
   paper, 6, 166, 183
Tape drive, 85, 166
Tape memory, 83, 85, 166, 182
Telephone coupler, 183
Teletype, 181
Terminal:
   printing, 6, 180
   smart, 165
   video, 6, 127, 165, 181
Texas Instruments 9900, 176
Timesharing, 7
Toggling, 127, 131
True, 25
Truth table, 26
2's complement, 100, 105
2650 microprocessor, 176

Variable:
   binary, 26
   dependent, 26
   independent, 26
   logic, 25
Video terminal, 6, 127, 165, 181
Volatile memory, 65, 79

Word, 66
   size of, 110, 164, 173
   structure of, 129
Word processing, 170
Write, 66

XOR, 32

Z-80 microprocessor, 175

Index

Zero, 9, 25
Zero check, 121
ZILOG Z-80, 175